The
Disappearing
Dictionary

David Crystal works from his home in Holyhead, North Wales, as a writer, editor, lecturer and broadcaster. He has published extensively on the history and development of English, including *The Stories of English, Evolving English* and *Spell It Out: The Singular Story of English Spelling*. He held a chair at the University of Reading for 10 years, and is now Honorary Professor of Linguistics at the University of Bangor. He was 'Master of Original Pronunciation' at Shakespeare's Globe in London for its productions of *Romeo and Juliet* and *Troilus and Cressida* in 2004–5, and has since acted as an accent consultant for other such productions worldwide. *The Disappearing Dictionary* is a companion to *You Say Potato: A Book About Accents* by Ben Crystal and David Crystal.

David Crystal

The
Disappearing
Dictionary

A treasury of lost English dialect words

MACMILLAN

First published 2015 by Macmillan
an imprint of Pan Macmillan
20 New Wharf Road, London N1 9RR
Associated companies throughout the world
www.panmacmillan.com

ISBN 978-1-4472-8280-8

3 5 7 9 8 6 4 2

A CIP catalogue record for this book is available from the British Library.

Map artwork by Kate Bellamy
Printed and bound by CPI Group (UK) Ltd, Croydon, CR0 4YY

Contents

A-Z

Exploring dialects

*alkitottle, batterfanged, cheeping-merry,
deepooperit, ernful . . .*

Why are dialects so fascinating? I've never met anyone who isn't intrigued by the extraordinary diversity of the English language, as it changes from place to place. Dialect words, in particular, capture the imagination. They give us an insight into the way people think who are both like us – in that they speak the same language – and yet not like us. And when we encounter old dialect words and expressions, it's like travelling back in time.

People who speak a regional dialect are usually very proud of the fact. This is because a dialect, like an accent, is a powerful expression of identity. An accent shows where you come from by the pronunciation you use. A dialect shows where you come from by the words and grammar you use. The two complement each other in this book, which celebrates Joseph Wright's magisterial *English Dialect Dictionary*.

Dialects are both national and international. British people notice the differences in the words Americans use, and vice versa. Cars/automobiles have boots/trunks and bonnets/hoods. But when people talk about dialect they usually mean the local variations in grammar and vocabulary within a country. 'Local' of course can mean many things. We can talk about the words that are used in a major political unit, such as Scotland or England, or within a major geographical area, such as 'the West Country', or within a particular county or city. Some words may be very local indeed, used only by people from a town or village. In the days when regular contact between communities was difficult, it was a natural consequence to find words and idioms emerging that were different from those used even a few miles down the road.

And nowhere was this diversity more apparent than in Britain. It's often said that there are more dialects in the British Isles than in any other part of the English-speaking world. We have to take such statements with a pinch of salt, because many parts of that world have had little or no dialect study at all. But Britain certainly takes some beating because of the range of influences on the development of the language over the past 1,500 years. The entries in this book show the varying impact on vocabulary of the Anglo-Saxon, Danish, and French invasions as well as of the indigenous Celtic communities. And there seems to be something special about the British readiness to engage in language play: many entries display a cheeky inventiveness in coining words and expressions. At times, it's almost as if localities were competing to see who could come up with the most idiosyncratic way of talking about something. Several of the items in this book reflect this irreverent, down-to-earth temperament.

The challenge facing any would-be dialectologist is thus immense. With such a long history, displaying such remarkable geographical diversity and periods of rapid change, where does one start? And how to devise a procedure to cover the country as a whole? The words and expressions are 'out there', certainly, but how to get at them? Enter Joseph Wright.

Joseph Wright

The story of Joseph Wright (1855–1930) begins in Thackley, a village north-east of Bradford in West Yorkshire. When he was six, he got a job driving a donkey-cart, carrying tools belonging to the stone-workers in nearby Shipley. The job, which stretched from seven in the morning till five at night, involved taking the tools to the nearest blacksmith's to be sharpened, and then bringing them back. It earned him eighteen pence a week, and he got an extra penny bonus from each quarryman.

A year later, his mother took him to a cotton mill – at the time, the largest one in Europe – which had been built by the philanthropic manufacturer Sir Titus Salt in 1853. Salt had created a model village for his workers which (being on the River Aire) he called Saltaire. Joseph was taken on half-time as a doffer in the spinning department. A doffer, according to the *English Dialect Dictionary*, was 'a boy or girl employed in a factory to remove the full bobbins from the throstle-frame [a spinning machine whose sound reminded people of a throstle – a song-thrush] and replace them by empty ones'. This was no menial task, as there were 144 spindles on each frame, and

over 16,000 on all the machines in the vast spinning shed (637 ft / 194 m long). He worked from 6 until 12.30 each morning, which meant an early start, as the mill was two miles from his home.

The other half of Wright's day was spent in a school that the enlightened Titus Salt provided for the children. It was the only school Wright ever attended, and – as he reflected later – it didn't teach him a great deal. He later wrote in *John o' London's Weekly* (15 May 1926): 'When I left school, I knew very little more than when I first went. I knew the alphabet, and had a smattering of elementary arithmetic, and I could recite, parrot-like, various Scriptural passages, and a few highly moral bits of verse; that was almost precisely the extent of my educational equipment after three or four years of schooling. Reading and writing, for me, were as remote as any of the sciences.' But, as he also liked to recall, the mill gave him a strong sense of local dialects, for the men came from all around the area.

He left Saltaire when he was thirteen and worked at a mill in Shipley, graduating to the more specialized work of wool-sorting, and stayed there for seven years. It was here, during his dinner-hour, that he taught himself to read and write, using just two books: the Bible and Bunyan's *Pilgrim's Progress*. His education progressed with a weekly purchase of Cassell's *Popular Educator* magazine, which became, as he put it, his 'constant companion'. Two or three evenings each week he went to a local night-school, where he began to learn French and

German. By the time he was twenty, he had taught himself Latin and learned shorthand.

He might have stayed a wool-sorter indefinitely, but in 1876 the mill had a temporary closure, so he used this as an opportunity to move on. Through his mill-work, along with some income from running a small night-school of his own, he had saved £40 – enough to pay for a term at a university. He chose Heidelberg, in Germany. On his return, he found work in Windhill as a schoolteacher, but his language interests motivated a return to Heidelberg in 1882, and there he began his studies as a philologist, eventually gaining a doctorate. He joined the university in Oxford in 1888, and produced a string of publications, culminating in his masterwork, the six-volume *English Dialect Dictionary*, published between 1898 and 1905, which he financed himself.

In later life Wright had to get used to eye-catching newspaper headlines – such as 'From Donkey-boy to Professor' – whenever he carried out a public engagement. Certainly, there is no other linguistic story quite as dramatic as the one in which an illiterate quarry-boy and mill-worker becomes a professor of comparative philology at Oxford University.

The English Dialect Dictionary

Nobody did more than Joseph Wright to lay the foundation for the study of English dialects. His dictionary is an impressively detailed account of the regional vocabulary of the British Isles at that time. It claims to be 'so far as is possible, the complete vocabulary of all dialect words which are still in use or are known to have been in use at any time during the last two hundred years in England, Ireland, Scotland, and Wales'. That's quite a claim, but the entries certainly support it. There had never been such detail provided on dialect usage before. And only the great Survey of English Dialects, half a century later, would surpass it.

It took Wright twenty-three years to collect all the material, and seven years to publish it. Volume 1, A–C, appeared in 1898. Volume 6, T–Z, along with various indexes and a Dialect Grammar, appeared in 1905. The scale of the project, in a pre-computer age, has to be appreciated. The entire work presents around 117,500 senses of words. Examples of usage are taken from over 3,000 dialect glossaries, works containing dialect words, and the contributions of over 600 voluntary readers and

A-PURPOSE, *adv.* Nhb. Wm. Lan. Oxf. Brks. [əpɔˑpəs, əpɔˑpəs.] On purpose, deliberately, with intention.]
Nhb.[1] He's deund aporpose to myek hissel leuk clivver. Wm.[1] Lan. O purpus fur to let foke get o seete on um, ORMEROD *Felley fro Rachde* (1851) i ; 'An accident done a-purpose,' chimed in Mrs. Clowes, BANKS *Manch. Man.* (1881) iv. Oxf.[1] He done it a-purpose, *MS. add.* Brks.[1] A drow'd [threw] I down a-purpose.
[*A*-, on + *purpose.*]

APURT, *adj.* and *adv.* Som. Dev. [əpɜ̂t.]
1. *adj.* Sulky, sullen, disagreeable.
n.Dev. B'ant bur well, Nan? Is our Nell apurt, ROCK *Jim an' Nell* (1867) st. 55 ; GROSE (1790) ; Apurt, with a glouting look, *Monthly Mag.* (1808) II. 431. Dev.[3] BRY. I can't go, zure.—RAB. Wull, very wull.—BRY. You be a-purt now, pt. i. 9 ; 'O,' quotha to dame, ' clumping eet ! so it ain you are a-purt with your meat,' pt. ii. 13.
2. *adv.* In a sulky manner ; disagreeably.
w.Som.[1] Her tookt her zel off proper apurt, and no mistake. nw.Dev.[1]
[*A*- (*pref.[2]*) + *purt* (to sulk), q.v.]

APURTED, *adj.* Dev. Sullen.
Dev. They only thought it was my ' appurted witherful develtry,' as they called it, MADOX-BROWN *Dwale Bluth* (1876) bk. iv. i.
[*A*- (*pref.[2]*) + *purted,* pp. of *purt,* see above.]

AQUABOB, *sb.* Ken. An icicle.
Ken. GROSE (1790) ; I have never heard this, and on inquiry cannot hear of it ; it looks rather like a fabrication (P.M.) ; Brks.[1]

AQUART, *adv.* Yks. Also written aquairt n.Yks.[3] [əkwɛˑrt, əkwɛ̂t.]
1. Across, athwart.
nn.Yks.[1] Used of motion across. T'beeos ran a-quart t'staggarth.
2. In a state of disagreement, at cross purposes.
n.Yks.[1] What, then, Marget an' her man hae getten aquart agen? —Ay, they's had another differing-bout ; n.Yks.[2] There's nought to get aquairt about. w.Yks. (Æ.B.)
[*A*-, on + *quart,* vb. (q.v.).]

AQUAT, *adv.[1]* Dor. Som. Also written aquott.
[əkwoˑt.] In a squatting position.
w.Dor. ROBERTS *Hist. Lyme Regis* (1834). e.Som. Aquat, sitting flat, like a bird on its eggs. W. & J. *Gl.* (1873). w.Som.[1] Steed o' treadin' the things there was he a-quat down in by the vire [xv. Quat].
[*A*-, on + *quat,* vb. (q.v.).]

AQUAT, *adv.[2]* Dev. Also written aquot Dev.[1] [əkwoˑt, əkwɛ̂t.] Full to satiety.
Dev. 'Chave eat so much 'cham quit a-quot [I have eat so much that I am cloyed], RAY (1691). n.Dev. I mind an alkitole o't Avore a month had got a-quot, ROCK *Jim an' Nell* (1867) st. 61 ; Aquot, weary of eating, GROSE (1790). Dev.[5] Willee's zome moar tō ayte, missis?—No thankee, vather, I be aquit now; party nigh vit tō bust.
[*A*- (*pref.[2]*) + *quat,* adv. (q.v.).]

AQUEESH, ACQUEESH, see Atweesh.
AR, see Air, *adj.,* Arr.
AR, see Ear.
ARAIN, *sb.* Dur. Yks. Lan. Der. Not. Also written arran Dur.[1] n.Yks. ne.Yks.[2] w.Yks.[5] ne.Lan.[1] ; aran n.Cy. w.Yks.[2] ; arrin Der.[2] nw.Der.[1] ; arrand, arand, arrant w.Yks. ; arrian w.Yks.[3] [əˑrɒnd, əˑroɒt, əˑrɒ, əˑriɒn.]
1. A spider, a cobweb.
n.Cy. GROSE (1790). Yks. At public worship the composure of a lady near him is much disturbed by an arrant, HAMILTON *Nugæ Lit.* (1841) 316; Arran, the long-legged outdoor spider (S.P.U.). w.Yks. Sweep'th Arrans down ; till all be clean, *keen* lin, Eh he'll leauk all Agyze, when he comes in, MERITON *Praise Ale* (1684) l. 43. w.Yks. Arran is used in this parish for spiders of every size, WATSON *Hist. Hfx.* (1775) 531 ; You never heard of Bruce, perhaps?—And th' arrand! BRONTË *Shirley* (1849) v; w.Yks.[2] Thoo hod as nice a bonny waist an onny body, as slim as an ensew, sigh, as an arran, ii. 297 ; An arran or an Espin leaf wad a fleaid him out of his witta, iii. 316 ; w.Yks.[2][3][4] ne.Lan.[1] Der.[2] The word arion was common in living memory, but has not been heard so much of late years ; Der.[3], nw.Der.[1] Not. Arain, used only for the larger kind of spiders, RAY (1691). [According to correspondents the word is now obs. in Notts.
2. *Comp.* Arain-web, Aran-web, a cobweb.
N.Cy.[2], Dur.[1], n.Yks.[2] n.Yks.[3] Arran-web, rarely used. w.Yks. It's better to be a bit blesterin an rough an have summat to show for it nor to caar in a corner wol th' arrand-webs stick to yo,

HARTLEY *Clock Alm.* (1896) 9 ; She had hair colour o' gowd, an' fine and silky as an arran-web, DIXON *Craven Dales* (1881) 189; w.Yks.[4] The infection of some fevers would stop in an arrinweb for seven years ; w.Yks.[5]
[Arain, large spider, COLES (1677) ; Oure ȝeris as the arane sall thynke . . The erayn makes vayn webbes, HAMPOLE *Ps.* lxxxix. 10; Oure ȝeris schulen bithenke as an ȝreyn, WYCLIF *ib.*; Aranye or erayne, *aranea,* *Prompt.* OFr. *araigne (iraigne),* Lat. *aranea,* a spider.]

ARB, see Herb.
ARBITRARY, *adj.* Hrf. Ken. Sur. Also written arbitry Hrf. Ken.[1] [ä·bitri.]
1. Independent, impatient of restraint.
Hrf. (W.W.S.) Sur.[1]
2. Hard ; greedy, grasping.
Ken.[1]

ARBOUR-TREE, see Harber.
ARBY-ROOT, same as Abby-root, q.v.
ARC, see Ark, *sb.[1]*
ARCG, see Argue.
ARCH, *sb.[1]* Sc. (JAM.) An aim. See Arch, *v.* 2
ARCH, *sb.[2]* Cor. Tech. A piece of ground left unworked near a shaft.
Cor. *Mining Gl.* (1852).
ARCH, *v.* Sc. Som. Cor. [ertʃ, ätʃ.]
1. To make or cause to be convex.
w.Som.[1] Thick there road must be a arched a good bit more eet, vore the water'll urn off vitty like.
2. To take aim, to throw or let fly any missile weapon with a design to hit a particular object.
Sc. Shoot again,—and O see to airch a wee better this time, *Brownie of Bodsbeck* I. 155 (JAM.). Abd. Airch, to throw, is still in use. It is (so called] from the curve described by a missile (G.W.). Rxb. (JAM.)
Hence **Arched,** *ppl. adj.* curved, convex, see 1; **Archer,** *sb.* (JAM.), one who throws, see 2; **Arching,** *adj.* convex, see 1.
Sc. The roads in a mine, when built with stones or bricks, are generally arched level drifts, *Mining Gl.* (1852). Tech. The roads in a mine, when built with stones or bricks, are sometimes called arched level or arched ways, WEALE *Dict. Terms* (1873). Abd. Archer, a marksman. w.Som.[1] He idn archin enough by ever zo much.
[OFr. *archer* (mod. *arquer*), to arch, to curve in the form of a bow (*arc*) ; a deriv. of *arc.*]

ARCH, see Argh.
ARCHANGEL, *sb.* [äˑkˑnᵍᵊl.]
1. A name applied to several species of Dead Nettle and allied plants :—(1) *Lamium album* (Lei. Glo. Dev.) ; (2) *Lamium galeobdolon* (Som.); (3) var. species of *Lamium* (Glo.).
Glo.[1] Dev. The harmless nettle is here [Dartmoor] called archangels, BRAY *Tamar and Tavy* (ed. 1879) I. 274 ; Dev.[4] w.Som.[1] Archangel, the yellow nettle, often called weazel snoot. [Our English archangels and a few others are yellow, *Cornh. Mag.* (Jan. 1880).]
2. Red Archangel, *Lamium purpureum* (Nrf.); Yellow Archangel, *Lamium galeobdolon* (Lei).
[Archangel, the name of a plant, called also Dead Nettle, JOHNSON ; Archangel (dead nettle), *Lamium,* COLES (1679) ; Ortie blanche, the herb Archangel, Blind Nettle, Dead Nettle. Ortie puante, a kind of Archangel that smells most filthily, COTGR. ; *Lamium album,* White Archangell. *Lamium luteum,* Yellow Archangell. *Lamium rubrum,* Red Archangell, GERARDE (ed. 1633) 702; Deffe nettylle, *Archangelus, Prompt.* ; *Archangelica,* the blynd netel, WRIGHT *Voc.* 565. 15.]

ARCHES, *sb. pl.* Tech. The first ' bungs of saggers,' or piles of clay boxes containing ware put into the oven.
Tech. In the pottery trade arches are the bungs which stand nearest to the fire and between the fire-holes or mouths, *Lsh. Gl.* (1894).

ARCH-HOLE, *sb.* Cum.
Cum.[1] Arch-whol, a vent-hole in the wall of a barn.
ARCHIE, see Urchin.

K 2

correspondents, all of whom of course had to be contacted by letter. Some entries were easy to manage: a single query about an individual word or phrase. Others were highly complex. A form researching dialect variations in the verb 'to be' asked correspondents to respond to 194 separate points. The information, as it came in, was handwritten onto slips. By the time Wright had completed his first volume, he had already accumulated 1.5 million slips.

An impression of the scale and level of detail of the project can be gained from the facsimile page (from which I took my entry on *apurt*). It shows the many quotations, sources, cross-references, pronunciations, etymologies, and variant spellings, along with the geographical locations in England, Wales, Scotland, or Ireland. It also gives an impression of the range of subject-matter, which included scientific data on regional plants and animals, as well as descriptions of technical notions in such areas as mining and agriculture, and accounts of popular games, customs, and superstitions. The vocabulary of just one children's game, marbles, runs to dozens of entries spread throughout the Dictionary.

Notwithstanding all this detail, it's important to appreciate the limitations of Wright's work. In particular, his geographical coverage reflects the dialect publications he consulted and the places where his correspondents lived. Some locations, such as Scotland and Yorkshire, get very detailed treatment as a result. In others, the treatment is much more sporadic. When Wright identifies *apurt* as being used in Devon and Somerset, for example, all this means is that he has hard evidence of it being used there. It doesn't mean it wouldn't have been used in Cornwall, or Dorset, or anywhere else. When reading the entries in his Dictionary, or those in the present book, it's important to appreciate that a usage may have been more widespread than he was able to discover. In the entries below, the regions listed immediately after the signpost symbol show where Wright found the headword in use. Any other regions mentioned within the entry refer to related words.

My selection

My aim in writing this book was twofold. First, I wanted to celebrate one of the greatest – yet most neglected – lexicographic achievements of modern times. Most people who have an interest in language know of the dictionaries compiled by Samuel Johnson, Noah Webster, and James Murray. Their stories have often been told, in textbooks and biographies. By contrast, few know of Wright's work, and fewer still have read the lovingly detailed memoir – long out of print – written by his wife Elizabeth in 1932. His dictionary is disappearing when it should be being remembered.

My other aim was to celebrate the dialects themselves. I find old words fascinating, especially when they express a notion in a vivid, playful, or ingenious way. Often they make us see things in a different light, or suggest an alternative way of talking about something to what is available in present-day English. Often it's simply the sound of the old word that captures the imagination. And always, there is the etymological question: how on earth did this word come to be used in this way? I've therefore chosen entries that illustrate the many different kinds of word and word history that are found in Wright's dictionary, but which are likely to be found in any dialect, ancient or modern.

I've also chosen words whose meaning is still relevant today. I didn't include words that reflected practices that have long died out – such as old street-games, legal systems, political parties, village customs, and farming methods – intriguing though these are in themselves. I thought it would be more interesting to find words that could still be used today, in relation to such topics as the weather, insults, everyday activities, types of personality, and states of mind. Indeed, in recent months I've found myself wanting to use several of these old words in conversation, simply because it seemed to suit the tone or mood of what I wanted to say better than any modern equivalent. Sometimes, indeed, there is no modern word that quite captures the nuance of the dialect form. I wouldn't be surprised to find that some of these old words achieve a new lease of life, as a consequence.

For this book, I've taken around 900 words and expressions from the dictionary and presented them in an alphabetical list of nearly 500 entries. My entries reflect Wright's balance of coverage. You will notice the large number of items under letter S, for example – 84 entries (18 per cent of the whole). This is because S is the largest letter in Wright's coverage, taking up a massive 700 pages of his Dictionary and including 20,450 entries (also 18 per cent).

I've kept Wright's headword spellings and definitions, and the quotations illustrating local usage are also in their original spelling. I haven't included all the spelling variations he noted, though, as there are simply too many. When people write down dialect pronunciations, they do so in all kinds of idiosyncratic ways. It's therefore often difficult to 'hear' the original accent through the spellings.

The only departure from his treatment has been to update his etymologies, insofar as more recent research has uncovered fresh historical relationships – though a surprising number of words are still 'etymology unknown'. I've also kept his geographical descriptions. The county names will not all be familiar, therefore, as nomenclature and political status have changed several times since the end of the nineteenth century. The maps on pages xxii–xxiii show the counties as they were in 1900.

A new lease of life? But perhaps some of these words haven't died out at all, and are still used or remembered in parts of the country. For every entry in this book, I found myself wondering: is the word really gone? And might it be known by readers from a different county than those mentioned by Wright? There are pages at the back of this book (and a website) for such encounters to be recorded. Dead or alive? That is the question.

Maps

The counties of England, Wales
and Scotland, 1900

ENGLAND

1. Bedfordshire
2. Berkshire
3. Buckinghamshire
4. Cambridgeshire
5. Cheshire
6. Cornwall
7. Cumberland
8. Derbyshire
9. Devon
10. Dorset
11. Durham
12. Essex
13. Gloucestershire
14. Hampshire
15. Herefordshire
16. Hertfordshire
17. Huntingdonshire
18. Isle of Wight
19. Kent
20. Lancashire
21. Leicestershire
22. Lincolnshire
23. Middlesex
24. Norfolk
25. Northamptonshire
26. Northumberland
27. Nottinghamshire
28. Oxfordshire
29. Rutland
30. Shropshire
31. Somerset
32. Staffordshire
33. Suffolk
34. Surrey
35. Sussex
36. Warwickshire
37. Westmoreland
38. Wiltshire
39. Worcestershire
40. Yorkshire

WALES

41. Cardigan
42. Glamorgan
43. Pembroke

SCOTLAND

1. Aberdeenshire
2. Ayrshire
3. Banffshire
4. Berwickshire
5. Dumfriesshire
6. Fife
7. Forfarshire (Angus)
8. Galloway (Wigtownshire)
9. Kirkcudbrightshire
10. Lanarkshire
11. Lothian
12. Orkney and Shetland Isles
13. Perthshire
14. Renfrewshire
15. Roxburghshire
16. Selkirkshire

Edinburgh

ISLE OF
MAN

A–Z

A

abbey-lubber (*noun*)

† Somerset, Yorkshire, and among sailors

An idle person, someone who loafs around. A 1679 dictionary pulled no punches: 'a slothful loiterer in a religious house under pretence of retirement and austerity'. Another early description is 'an arch-frequenter of the cloister beef-pot', summing it up in the very fine coinage: *archimarmitonerastique*. And yes, there is a link with the ('Love it, Hate it, Just don't forget it') Marmite. A *marmite* was a metal cooking-pot – an image still seen on jars of that foodstuff.

abundation (*noun*)

† Cheshire, Gloucestershire, Herefordshire, Shropshire, Staffordshire, Worcestershire

A great quantity. John Wycliffe's Bible popularized the new word (in the fourteenth century) *abundance*. *Abundation* seems to have emerged later as a down-market alternative, especially for situations where things aren't

3

going right. We read of a Cheshire man bemoaning the lack of turnips while 'we shan have abundation o'teetoes'. It carries echoes of *inundation*.

aclite (*adverb*)
Northumberland, Scotland

Awry, out of joint. The Tyneside poet Robert Gilchrist lamented the loss to Newcastle of the death of a beloved character in 'Blind Willie's Epitaph':

> *Newcastle's now a dowdy place – all things
> seem sore aclite,*
> *For here at last Blind Willie lies, an honest,
> harmless wight.*

adawds (*adverb*)
Yorkshire

In pieces. You'd usually hear it in the phrase 'rive all adawds' – to tear something into little bits. A *dawd* or *dad* was widely used across the North of England and up into Scotland to mean a lump or chunk of something. People would talk about 'a dad o' bread' or 'dawds o' cheese' – or even 'dawds o' common sense'. *Adawds* was recorded only in Yorkshire by Joseph Wright, also in the spelling *adauds*, but it was probably widespread further north.

addle (*adjective*)

🕇 Herefordshire, Kent, Norfolk, Suffolk, Surrey, Sussex

Unwell, ailing; tumble-down, loose, shaky. Only eggs and brains seem to be addled these days. In earlier times, it could be most things. From Sussex: 'My little girl seemed rather addle this morning' – so she didn't go to school. Anything in a rickety condition might be described as *addle*. From Kent: 'Dat waggin be turrble addle'. The word meant 'slime' or 'piss' in Old English.

afflufe (*adverb*)

🕇 Scotland

Extempore, without premeditation. The word, often written *aff loof*, was chiefly used to describe someone telling a story spontaneously, from memory – 'off book'. *Loof* was an old North Country word, borrowed from Old Norse, for the palm of a hand – hence the meaning of 'off hand' (which became 'offhand'). A normal process for speech, it had risky implications when used in other contexts. 'Whene'er I shoot wi' my air gun', writes a man in 1789, ''Tis ay aff loof'. People kept well away from him.

afflunters *see* **flunter**

a-goggle (*adjective*)

† Berkshire, Hampshire

Trembling. *Agog* these days is all to do with excitement and expectation, but in some dialects it had the meaning of being 'on the move'; and when part of one's body was repeatedly on the move – as with involuntary shaking during an illness – the frequency was neatly captured by *a-goggle*. 'His head is all a-goggle', someone might say. The word seems to have died out in this sense – presumably because *goggle* developed a more dominant meaning to do with staring eyes.

ainish *see* hainish

aizam-jazam (*adjective*)

† Gloucestershire, Shropshire, Staffordshire, Warwickshire, Worcestershire

Equitable, fair and square. The spelling varies greatly. From Worcestershire, of a dishonest bargain: 'That job's not quite aizam-jaizam'. From Staffordshire: 'I shouldn't care if he'd only act hasum-jasum with me'. The origin seems to be a form of *easy* in its sense of 'even' – a sense still around today, as when we say *I'm easy*, meaning 'I don't mind either way'. The doubled form intensified the meaning, much as it does in *easy-peasy*.

alag (*adverb*)

Cumberland, Northumberland, Yorkshire

Not sufficiently perpendicular. Ladders against walls could be described as *alag*. But more often, the word had a negative implication. From Northumberland: 'It's all alag'. From Yorkshire: 'It lies alag'. Doubtless the contributors were thinking of a failed attempt at DIY shelving.

alkitotle *or* alcatote (*noun*)

Devon

A foolish fellow. 'Go, ya alkitotle!' writes Peter Lock, the author of *Exmoor Scolding*, in 1768. Here's the full title of his book:

> *An Exmoor Scolding, in the Propriety and Decency of Exmoor Language, between Two Sisters, Wilmot Moreman & Thomasin Moreman, as They Were Spinning. . . . Together with Notes, and a Vocabulary For explaining uncouth Expressions, and interpreting barbarous Words and Phrases.*

And, for the record, a sample of the exchange:

> Wilmot: ya purling, tatchy, stertling, joweriiig, prinking, mincing theng!
> Thomasin: ya gurt chonnting, grumbling, glumping, zower-sapped, yerring trash!

It goes on like that for pages. Like *alkitotle*, the origin of many scolding words is lost in the mists of time.

all-overish (*adjective*)

† Berkshire, Cornwall, Derbyshire, Lancashire, Lincolnshire, Somerset, Warwickshire

Slightly out of sorts, nervous. From Warwickshire: a man complains of feeling 'All-overish, queer-like' – going down with something. But you can be well and still feel all-overish, especially when you hear some unpalatable news, find yourself in a threatening situation, or encounter an uncomfortable topic, as with this Cornishman: 'There's a kind of what-I-can't-tell-'ee about dead men that's very enticin', tho' it do make you feel all-overish'.

alunt (*adverb*)

† Scotland

In a blazing state. A *lunt* was a lighted match or pipe, or something you would use for lighting (a fire or the fuse of a firework or gun). Flames leaping up would be *lunting*. So would someone walking along smoking. The word arrived from Dutch in the sixteenth century, and was later adapted to states of mind: 'Sweet Meg maist set my saul alunt', writes a Scottish poet in 1811.

amplush (*noun*)

† Ireland, Wales

A disadvantage, state of unreadiness. From Pembrokeshire: 'I did'n expect it, a took me all on a umplush'. *An amplush* also turns up as *a namplush* – the kind of mix-up we often see in the history of English, as with *adder* coming from *a naddre*, or *apron* from *a napron* (see also *attercop*, *nazzard*). *Amplush* may be a version of *nonplus* – as in 'I was nonplussed'.

anguishous (*adjective*)

Cheshire, Lancashire

Painful, or sorrowful – but much stronger. From Lancashire: 'He lookt quite anguishous, an aw felt sorry for him'. The word works in both directions: something that causes anguish, or the feeling that results from being fraught with anguish. It's an ancient word, dating from the thirteenth century, when it arrived in English from French, expressing something stronger than just *anxious* or *distressed*.

aptish *or* eptish (*adjective*)

Yorkshire

Skilful, quick-witted. This is *apt* meaning 'ready to learn', rather than 'suitable' or 'appropriate'. From North Yorkshire: 'He's eptish at his book-lear'. But the word could also be used for things: people might talk about a tool being *aptish* for a particular job. Don't read in the meaning of *-ish* as 'somewhat' (as in *brownish*). Think of it along with words where the meaning is 'truly resembling', such as *boyish* and *sluggish*.

apurt (*adjective or adverb*)

Devon, Somerset

Sulky, disagreeable; in a sulky manner. From Somerset: 'Her tookt her zel [self] off proper apurt, and no mistake'. *Purt* meaning 'sulk' was widely used in south-west England: someone might be called 'a purting glum-pot', for instance, and if you put on a sulky face, you were *gone purt*. Decaying potatoes were *gone purt* too. The origin isn't clear, but there may be a relationship with *pout*.

argh (*adjective or adverb*)

Durham, Lincolnshire, Northumberland, Scotland, Sussex, Yorkshire

Fearful, apprehensive. This is one of the unusual *gh* spellings where the pronunciation developed into [f], as in *enough*, and the word is indeed often spelled with an *f* in dialect writing. From Aberdeenshire: 'I have an eargh kind of feeling on hearing the owls'. From Lincolnshire: 'I'm arf you've hurted the bunny'. The word could also mean 'insufficient' or 'scanty', and this led to its common use as an adverb when telling the time, as in Roxburgh: 'It's erfe twal o'clock' – almost twelve. There was a noun, too: *arghness*, meaning 'timidity' or 'reluctance'. It all goes back to an Old English word for 'cowardly'.

argle (*verb*)

Durham, Lincolnshire, Scotland, Warwickshire, Worcestershire

Argue. The pronunciation shift totally changes the feel of this word, making it sound more like its meaning, like *haggle* and *niggle*. Indeed, the word might originally have come from a confusion with *haggle*, for it was often used to describe bargaining with someone. Then it reduplicated. An *argle-bargle* was an argument (like *argie-bargie*). An *argle-bargler* was a really argumentative type. And if you were really quarrelsome, you were *argol-bargolous*.

arse-verse (*noun*)

Scotland, Yorkshire

Despite its appearance, this has nothing to do with one's rear end. It was a spell written on the side of a house to ward off fire – and sometimes witchcraft. The *arse* part comes from a Latin word meaning 'burn' – seen today in *arson*.

arsle (*verb*)

Cumberland, Lancashire, Norfolk, Suffolk, Yorkshire

Move backwards – from a Dutch word, *aarzelen*, which probably arrived in England via the trade routes between Holland and East Anglia. In Norfolk, a timid boxer was described as someone who 'kept arseling backwards, and durst not meet his man'. If you were 'arseling about' while sitting down, you were fidgeting. These days, it would be impossible to use the word without the buttocks making their presence felt, especially as they seem to be involved in these senses. But etymologically it's just a coincidence.

ashiepattle (*noun*)

Ireland, Scotland

From the days when real fires burned in homes – a child or domestic animal that lounges or works about the hearth, and thus gets covered with ash. The word is probably from *ash-pit*, with the *-le* adding a diminutive nuance – 'little one' – but with a tone of disgust rather than endearment. It seems to have been most often used in the very north of Scotland, in the Orkneys and Shetlands, and in Ireland it turns up as *ashiepelt* and *ashypet*. Cinderella was an *ashypet*.

attercop (*noun*)

Cheshire, Cumberland, Ireland, Lancashire, Northumberland, Scotland, Westmorland, Wiltshire, Yorkshire

An ill-natured or petulant person. An *attercop* was a spider, or a spider's web. It's an Old English word: *attor* was poison, and *cop*, from *coppa*, was a round head. *Coppa* itself seems to have been used alone for a spider, hence *cop-web* – or *cobweb*, as we say today. In the Middle Ages, *attercop* turns up applied to people, and seems to have been used in this way all over northern England and especially in Scotland. In Chapter 64 of *Waverley*, Walter Scott describes a character as 'a fiery etter-cap'. In Lancashire, the word turns up as *natter-crop*, having stolen the *n* from a preceding *an* (see also *amplush*, *nazzard*).

awf (*noun*)

Cheshire, Derbyshire, Lancashire, Scotland, Shropshire, Staffordshire, Wales, Warwickshire, Yorkshire

Originally, an elf's child, a changeling left by the fairies – thus any abnormal child, and so into dialect as an insult for anyone thought to be a fool or half-wit, equivalent to *oaf* in standard English. 'Tha great awf' would have been heard all over the Midlands and the North of England, with echoes in Wales and Scotland too. Perhaps it's still heard. *Awf* is one of those punchy, monosyllabic words beloved of English speakers when they want to insult someone, and I'd be surprised if it had totally disappeared.

awvish (*adjective or adverb*)

Cheshire, Derbyshire, Durham, Lancashire, Staffordshire, Warwickshire, Yorkshire

Slightly unwell, out of sorts. From Yorkshire: 'I feel myself queer and awvish'. And in a related sense, we see it meaning 'reluctant' or 'undecided': one might be very *awvish* about doing something. In Lancashire, if you were being really perverse, you could be accused of *awvishness*. The *awf* element is probably a pronunciation variant of *half*. You had to watch the context carefully, as there was another *awvish* around, meaning 'silly' or 'mischievous'. From Cheshire: 'He's so awvish when he's in drink'. From Lancashire: 'Keep out of his road, aw tell thi; he's an awvish nowty felly'. That had a different origin, from *elf*.

B

backsyfore (*adjective or adverb*)

🕇 Cornwall, Devon, Shropshire

The wrong side first. From Devonshire: 'Thee hast a' put on thy hat backsivore'. But the word goes well beyond the modern sense of 'back-to-front'. It could also mean 'the contrary way', as in this example from Cornwall: 'Wemmen be oogly things ef you rub 'em backsyfore'. And the meaning of 'clumsy' is dominant in 'A cruel backsyvore job he'th a-made o't', from Devon. It must have been a popular expression, for it gave birth to *backsyforemost* and the rhyming *backsyforsy*. A *backsyforsy side* of something would be a rear view.

baggerment (*noun*)

🕇 Lincolnshire

Rubbish. The word applied both to worthless talk – 'He talked a lot of baggerment' – and worthless things – 'Your land is full of baggerment'. A variant form was *bagment*, which led to the adjective *bagmentally*, meaning 'worthless' – 'He's a bagmentally chap'. The origin seems to be *baggage*, which developed the sense of 'rubbish' during the sixteenth and seventeenth centuries, echoed today in such expressions as *emotional baggage* and *intellectual baggage* – 'undesirable beliefs or experiences carried around in one's head'.

baltiorum (*noun*)

 Yorkshire

Boisterous merry-making which often accompanies a bonfire – and thus, any kind of riotous proceedings. It's a playful mock-Latin coinage, with the ending seen in such other colloquialisms as *cockalorum* ('a self-important little man') and *jiggalorum* ('a trifle'). The *bal-* part is a puzzle, though. It might be an echo of *hullabaloo*. *Baloo* was recorded on its own, meaning 'uproar', in places as far apart as Devon and Northamptonshire.

bamfoozle (*verb*)

Cornwall, Somerset, Yorkshire

Deceive, confuse, especially by trickery. *Bamboozle* is the more widely used word, and *bamfoozle* is obviously an adaptation – perhaps showing the influence of *confuse*. It probably arose at the same time, in the early seventeenth century. In an essay for the *Tatler* magazine in 1710, Jonathan Swift lists *bamboozle* as one of the new slang coinages 'struggling for the vogue' in London. Country folk hearing the strange word would easily have misheard or mispronounced it.

bange (*noun or verb*)
🕆 Essex, Hertfordshire, Norfolk, Suffolk

Fine rain, drizzle. The word rhymes with *range*. And to describe what's happening to the weather? *Bangy.* 'Tis a bangy morning', they used to say in that part of the world, and perhaps some still do.

bangster (*noun*)
🕆 Scotland

A bully, a violent fellow – one of several words that come from *bang*, in its sense of 'strike'. If you were *bangsome* or *bangie* you were really quarrelsome. Like it or not, bangsters often won the day – hence its other meaning of 'victor'. Walter Scott uses the word in this sense in Chapter 19 of *The Abbot*: a fight breaks out after someone insults the Pope in an alehouse, and is beaten for his pains, leading an onlooker to say: 'If the Pope's champions are to be bangsters in our very change-houses, we shall soon have the old shavelings back again' – the monks will be back!

barkle (*verb*)

Derbyshire, Lancashire, Lincolnshire,
Northumberland, Nottinghamshire, Yorkshire

Cake, encrust (with dirt) – said especially of hair, skin, and clothes. From Lincolnshire: 'I was that barkled wi' muck when I com oot of Cleugh Heäd, I thoht I should niver get mysen cleän no moore'. The notion is of someone being covered with dirt as bark covers a tree. D. H. Lawrence liked to use it: in Chapter 12 of *Sons and Lovers* we find Paul and Clara climbing down a steep path of red clay: 'Their barkled shoes hung heavy on their steps'.

bathy (*adjective*)

Gloucestershire, Kent, Shropshire, Worcestershire

Damp, moist – said especially of food, grass, and domestic linen. The word reflects the pronunciation of *bathe* not *bath*. Grass-cutting was especially affected, as a Gloucestershire writer records: 'The grass is that bathy, as it bawds the scythe' – fouls it up.

batterfanged (*adjective*)

Lincolnshire, Yorkshire

Bruised, beaten, scratched – as if 'battered by fangs'. From Lincolnshire: 'Hed been a so'dger i' th' Roosian war, an' come hoäme reg'lar batterfanged'. To get 'a good batterfanging' was to receive a severe clawing, whether from an animal or a human, as a Yorkshire writer sedately records: 'The consequences, in the shape of combined blows and scratches, which await the champion who engages a female combatant in battle'.

bazzock (*verb*)

 Yorkshire

Beat, thrash. The spelling varies greatly, including *bazzack* and *bassock*. In a Yorkshire story, we read: 'He bazzacked her whahl she was stiff as a stowp' – until she was stiff as a post. And in another place a man gets 'a good bazzicking'. Several words could be related to the first part, such as *bash* and *baste*. The *-ock* ending has a wide range of meanings in English, usually to do with things being small (*hillock*, *bollock*) or clumpy (*hummock*, *tussock*), but here it seems to have an intensifying force, as with *mammock* – 'tear to pieces'.

beflum (*verb*)

 Scotland, Yorkshire

Deceive by using cajoling language. In Walter Scott's *The Bride of Lammermoor* (Chapter 25), Caleb escapes from just such a situation: 'An [if] I had been the Lord High Commissioner to the Estates o' Parliament, they couldna hae beflumm'd me mair'. This is *be-* in the sense of 'affecting someone or something', as when one is *befriended*, but here with a nuance of 'thoroughly'. The *flum* part is probably a shortened form of *flummox*, widely used in dialects before it became part of standard colloquial English.

begrumpled (*adjective*)

⸶ Cornwall, Devon, Somerset

Displeased, affronted. There's something about *gr-* that suggests a gloomy state of mind: think of *grumble*, *grumpy*, *growl*, *grim*, and other such words. *Grump*, as a verb meaning 'complain constantly', was used all over England. From Worcestershire: 'er sits and grumps'. If you *took the grump* you would have lost your temper. In Scotland a surly person was said to be *grumply*. *Begrumpled* fits into this family well, with the *be-* prefix adding a note of 'very much'.

begunk (*verb*)

⸶ Cumberland, Ireland, Scotland

Cheat, deceive, jilt. And *begunked*: cheated, disappointed. There may be a link with *geck*, from Dutch, meaning 'fool', but the sound effect of the *-unk* ending (as in *clunk* and *kerplunk*) gives the word a no-nonsense finality that's lacking in its standard English counterparts. Which is the more definite: 'I've been jilted' or 'I'm clean begunk'?

bemoil (*verb*)

Lincolnshire, Staffordshire, Worcestershire

Covered in mud – from a French verb meaning 'drench' or 'soak'. The word was probably known in Warwickshire too, judging by the way Shakespeare used it in Act 4 Scene 1 of *The Taming of the Shrew*. Grumio describes how Katherina fell off her horse in a really muddy place – 'how she was bemoiled'.

bencher (*noun*)

Worcestershire

An idler at a public house. 'Thee be'st a riglar bencher, thee'st weared thy breeches out a sittin' o' the public-'ouse bench'. The word was also applied to other bench-sitting situations, especially in the legal profession, and became part of standard English, but it never lost its original tavern use.

beraffled (*adjective*)

Yorkshire

Perplexed, entangled. 'Ah's sair beraffled what te deea' – what to do. It's the notion of entanglement that points to the word's origin, where there seems to be a link with the random elements seen in a pile of *raff* ('rubbish') or a *riff-raff* ('rabble') – words which came into English from French in the fifteenth century. It can indeed be a perplexing business, sorting out a tangle of odds and ends.

betwattled (*adjective*)

Cornwall, Cumberland, Devon, Lancashire, Northamptonshire, Northumberland, Somerset, Yorkshire

Confused, bewildered. The word turns up all over the country in a remarkable variety of forms – *betrattlt* in Cumberland; *bewottled* in Northamptonshire; *betotled* and *bedwadled* in Devon; *bewattled* in Cornwall. From Yorkshire: 'Ah's fairly betwattled and baffounded'. The root, *twattle*, clearly has its place in a family of echoic words all expressing a notion of 'foolish talk' or 'gossip', and looks like a blend of *twaddle* and *tittle-tattle*. An interesting extension was recorded in North Yorkshire: if you were betwattled there, you were hardly sober.

betwittered (*adjective*)

Corkshire

Excited, frightened – anything, in fact, which might cause you to *twitter*, meaning 'tremble'. Joseph Wright adds the gloss 'overcome with pleasing excitement', bringing his entry on this word up to 130 characters (including spaces), and thereby anticipating another possible application a century later.

birthy (*adjective*)

🪧 Ireland, Northumberland, Scotland

Numerous, prolific. From Northern Ireland: 'Them beans is very birthy'. Potatoes were described as birthy too, if they had a good number of tubers at each stalk. All the recorded instances seem to be agricultural. An ideal word for exhibits at County Shows.

blaff (*noun or verb*)

🪧 Scotland

To go bang, or the bang that results. Guns went blaff, as did dogs ('bark'), but a blaff was also a blow, physical or otherwise. In Chapter 2 of Samuel Rutherford Crockett's *The Men of the Moss-Hags* (1895), two women are fleeing from sheep-stealers, and have a tough ride home without mishap, but then one is wounded when almost at their house. She wryly observes: 'Tha hardest blaff of down-come is ever gotten at the doorstep'. Very true.

blashy (*adjective*)

🪧 Cumberland, Durham, Ireland, Leicestershire, Lincolnshire, Northamptonshire, Northumberland, Scotland, Warwickshire, Yorkshire

Rainy, gusty; wet, muddy; weak, watery; frivolous, over-talkative. The weather, roads, fields, ale, tea, and conversation could all be blashy. *Splash* lies behind all these senses, for an interesting phonetic reason. When *splash* is spoken, the *s* makes the *p* change its normal character (technically, it loses its aspiration), so that it sounds more like a *b*. The first three senses are fairly obvious developments; the fourth is unexpected, though to think of frivolity as someone splashing around in speech or behaviour is rather appealing.

blawp (*noun and verb*)

 Scotland

Belch, burp. This is simply a contracted form of *blow up*, with the open Scots vowel shown by the *aw* spelling. I don't think there's any connection with *Blawp*, the alien digital character created by Jim Henson's Creature Shop for the 1998 film *Lost in Space*, but I might be wrong.

blodder (*verb*)

 Westmorland

Of liquor: to flow with a gurgling sound out of a vessel with a narrow aperture, such as a beer or wine bottle. 'It's o' bloddered away oot o' t'bottle'. There may be a link with *blood*. It turns up as *blutter* in Scotland. It was also used when someone (especially a child) was crying excessively: 'What for is thoo blodderin an rooarin?' What's not clear is which came first – the liquor or the kids.

bluify (*verb*)

† Hertfordshire

To become blue. 'My hands are quite blueified with the cold'. The *-ify* suffix has a long history of making verbs from adjectives, all expressing the idea of 'bringing into a certain state', as with *horrify* and *stupify*. The coinages have often been playful or jocular, as with *speechify*. But *bluify* evidently met a need. I wonder just how many other colours were treated in the same way? There's no dialect record of a *yellowify* or *greenify*, yet.

blup (*noun*)

† Scotland

A misfortune brought on through lack of foresight. If you have been *blupt*, you've been overtaken by a misfortune that you might have avoided if you'd been more cautious. In Lothian, anyone making a clumsy or awkward appearance was also called a *blup*. There are echoes in *blooper* and *muppet*.

blutterbunged (*adjective*)

† Lincolnshire

Overcome by surprise – so that no talk (*blather*) can come out (because you're 'bunged up' with the emotion of the occasion). In 1890 Wright reports a story of a preacher in a chapel who had just spoken the biblical text 'Behold, the

Bridegroom cometh' when in walked a newly married couple. This so put him off that he exclaimed: 'Well, mi brethren, I'm clean blutterbunged!'

bobbersome (*adjective*)

Cheshire, Lancashire, Northumberland, Shropshire, Westmorland, Yorkshire

In high spirits, bold, forward, impatient. From Shropshire: 'Dunna yo be too bobbersome wi' yore money'. The word could be a compliment or a criticism. One Lancashire writer is delighted with his new cap: 'isn't it bobbersome!' Another finds being compared to a hedgehog is 'a bit too bobbersome'. *Bob* is the source of the word, with its meaning of 'move quickly up and down' transferred to a state of mind.

bodderment *see* botherment

bogfoundered (*adjective*)

Cheshire

Perplexed, bewildered. According to the *Altrincham Guardian* in 1896, a woman said 'she was bogfoundered in the matter' – swallowed up in a bog. *Bog* was used in this part of the country to mean a dilemma or quandary: 'Oo towd [you told] me th' same thing o'er and o'er again till a wur aw [I were all] in a bog'.

boldrumptious (*adjective*)

🕈 Kent

Presumptuous. A blend of *bold* and *rumpus*, along with the -*ious* ending, meaning 'full of', seen in such words as *fictitious* and (strongly echoed here) *bumptious*. Or maybe the ending was the -*uous* heard in *presumptuous*, but mispronounced. Either way, it resulted in a forceful expression, as here: 'That there upstandin' boldrumptious blousing [wild] gal of yours came blarin' down to our house'.

bombaze *see* **bumbaze**

boneshave (*noun*)

🕈 Devon, Somerset

Sciatica. The *shave* part is an old use of this word to mean 'scrape' or 'chafe'. Exmoorians used to try to charm it away, hoping water would carry the disease down to the sea. Affected people had to lie on their back on the bank of a stream, with a straight staff by their side between them and the water, while these words were repeated over them:

> Bone-shave right,
> Bone-shave strite [= straight],
> As tha watter rins by tha stave,
> Zo follow bone-shave.

Worth a try, but in the case reported by Joseph Wright the sufferer died the next day.

boodyankers (*interjection*)

Northumberland

An exclamation of surprise or delight. The etymology is unclear, but there are echoes of *boo*, used to surprise or give a fright. Perhaps *boody* was an avoidance of *bloody*. The ending sounds playful. It beats *gosh*, no question.

botherment *or* **bodderment** (*noun*)

Cumberland, Devon, Somerset, Westmorland, Yorkshire

Trouble, difficulty. It seems in these parts of the country there was a need for something in between the mildness of *bother* and the forcefulness of *botheration*, which was so strong that it was often used as an exclamation. Judging by this Cumberland example, it was quite a punchy word: 'A heap eh balderdash an bodderment'. Or this one from Westmorland: 'I want nin o' thi bodderment'.

boundsy (*adjective or noun*)

Yorkshire

Said of someone who is stout and unusually active when walking, so that one notices the person's size. The word presumably wasn't entirely complimentary, as the -*sy* suffix is usually associated with a tone of mockery or dismissiveness, as in *artsy-fartsy* and *folksy*. The *bound* part reflects the girth, not the exercise. As an adjective, in this part of the country, *bound* meant 'of large circumference' (compare *boundary*). A lady wearing a large hooped petticoat could be described as 'boundsy'.

bowdykite (*noun*)

Durham, Northumberland, Yorkshire

A corpulent person. A *bowdy*, in Northumberland, was a large wooden bowl, and the *kite*, a bird of prey, was often used to describe someone who was greedy – hence the compound for a 'fatty' (all the recorded examples refer only to men). From Yorkshire: 'Off he set, as hahd as ivver his bowdykite legs wad carry him'. Rather less obvious was *bowdykite* as a term of contempt for a forward or precocious child, especially one behaving stupidly. There may be echoes of 'bighead' – *bowden* is recorded further north with the meaning of 'swollen'.

bowzelly (*adjective*)

Scotland, Sussex

Unkempt, tangled – pronounced 'boozly'. A contributor from Selkirkshire talks of 'bowzelly hair', where it seems to mean 'bushy', and an adaptation of *bushy* could be the origin. On the other hand, there was a verb *bowze* used in parts of Scotland and the North of England meaning 'rush' (like the wind) or 'gush forth', so that's a possible origin too.

brabagious (*adjective*)

Scotland, Sussex

Cantankerous. 'You nasty brabagious creature' turns up in the middle of a Sussex argument. The word probably comes from *brabble*, widely used across the Midlands and North of England to mean a quarrel. In Act 4 Scene 8 of Shakespeare's *Henry V*, the Welsh Captain Fluellen advises a soldier: 'keep you out of prawls, and prabbles, and quarrels' – his Welsh accent appearing in the *p*- spellings.

brackle (*adjective*)

Lancashire, Lincolnshire, Norfolk, Northamptonshire, Staffordshire, Suffolk, Yorkshire

Brittle, crumbling. In its agricultural sense, referring to stems of wheat that snap off short, *brackle* – related to *break* – wouldn't be of general interest. But it didn't stop there. Weather that was unsettled came to be described as *brackle* – or, in some places, *brockle* or *bruckle*. But whatever the pronunciation, a 'brackle day' would be one where calm weather was breaking up around you. 'Right brackly today', you might say.

braddled (*adjective*)

Leicestershire

Comfortably warmed through. 'You're nicely braddled!' – said to a child whose feet had been held near the fire. It's from an Old English verb meaning 'to roast'.

briss (*noun*)

Devon, Somerset

Dust and fluff that accumulates behind furniture. There's probably a distant relation to *break*, and a closer one to Irish English, where *briss* meant 'broken pieces' or 'little bits' (from the Gaelic verb *bris*, 'break'). From Somerset: 'Clean up all this briss behind the picture'. If the dust has accumulated along with the bits and pieces caught in cobwebs, it was *briss and buttons*. Why buttons? The phrase was also used for sheep's droppings. Today *briss* would gain a second lease of life to describe the gunk that accumulates between the keys on a computer keyboard.

brittner (*noun*)

Westmorland, Yorkshire

A term of commendation for a clever, active, or useful man or boy. From Yorkshire: 'Set thy shoodher tiv it, an push like a brittner'. Like a Briton.

broggle (*verb*)

Ireland, Lancashire, Lincolnshire, Scotland, Westmorland, Yorkshire

Push with a pointed instrument, poke. *Brog* was used in Scotland and the North Country with this meaning, and *broggle* seems to add a nuance of repeated action. From Lincolnshire: 'You're alus [always] brogglin' at th' fire; noä wonder it can't bo'n [burn]'. A *broggle* was an ineffectual attempt, and a *broggler* someone who tried and failed – a bungler.

broodle *(verb)*

† Devon, Lincolnshire, Shropshire

Let a child lie till quite awake. From Devon, of a child just waking up: 'Purty thing, it hathn't broodled yet'. The source is the farmyard: a hen brooding over her chickens. But anyone sitting in a meditative way might be said to be broodling.

bruff *(adjective)*

† Ireland, Kent, Lancashire, Norfolk, Suffolk, Sussex, Westmorland, Worcestershire, Yorkshire

Well and hearty, in appearance and manners; somewhat rough and blunt in manner. In other words, if someone said you were bruff, you'd have no idea whether they were being nice or nasty, without seeing their face and noting the context. The same ambiguity was found with *bluff*, from which it probably derives.

buck-thwanging *or* -swanging *(noun)*

† Lancashire, Yorkshire

The punishment of swinging a person against a wall. An old meaning of *swing* was 'throw with force', and from that developed a verb *swang*, 'to swing to and fro'. A *thwang* was a 'blow'. And *buck* reflects the action of a deer leaping from the ground and arching its back. Whatever the etymology, the result must have been quite painful. Apparently it was used in some trades when a worker was thought to have let his fellows down – such as by being lazy or drunk.

buldering (*adjective*)

Cornwall, Devon, Somerset

Of weather or the sky: threatening, thundery, sultry. A Devonshire spelling suggests its origin: 'Great bouldering clouds' – like boulders. *Buldery* and *boldery* were used in the same way. From Somerset: 'We shall have rain avore long, looks so buulduree' – the double *u* suggesting the pronunciation 'bool-dry'.

bumbaze *or* bombaze (*verb*)

Norfolk, Northumberland, Scotland, Suffolk

Bewilder, look aghast. From Northumberland: 'Aw was fairly bumbazed, like a dog in a dancin'. There was a verb *baze*, meaning 'astonish', which came into English from Dutch, and *bumbaze* could be a playful, resonant intensifying of that. But it has echoes of *bamboozle* and *amaze* too. All the recorded examples show it to have been a forceful expression, often reinforced by a word meaning 'absolutely'. From Ayrshire: 'clean bumbazed'. From Norfolk: 'right on bombazed'.

buzgut (*noun*)

🪧 Cornwall

A great eater or drinker. The first part has nothing to do with 'buzzing', even though it sounds as if it does. It's from an Old Cornish word for 'food'.

buzznacking (*verb or noun*)

🪧 Cumberland, Devon, Somerset, Yorkshire

Fussing, gossiping. It seems to be a blend of *buzz*, meaning 'gossip, tell tales', and *knack*, 'chatter' – so anyone buzznacking is really going on and on. But *knack* could also mean 'talk in an affected way, copying educated, southern speech'. From North Yorkshire: 'She knacks and knappers [rattles on] like a London miss'. Such accents were often criticized locally. From Cumberland: 'She knacks and talks like rotten sticks'. (*Knack* could also mean snap or crack.)

C

cabby (*adjective*)

† Buckinghamshire, Cornwall, Devon, Somerset

Sticky, dirty, muddy. From Devon: 'The road's cruel cabby after the rain'. But it could also be used for the weather itself, especially if humid and clammy: 'A proper cabby day'. In Cornwall, anything untidy could be described as *cabby*, as could a clumsy person. A very useful word, in short, from *cab*, meaning 'a sticky mess'.

cabobble (*verb*)

† Cornwall, Norfolk, Suffolk

To mystify, puzzle, confuse. From Cornwall: ''T'ull niver do for ee to try to cabobble Uncle Zibidee'. It's probably a jocular coinage that caught on – as with some other words for mental states that express the notion of disturbance by using the 'movement' suggested by *bob*, such as *discombobulate*.

cackle-stomached (*adjective*)

Worcestershire

Squeamish, over-particular, having an easily disgusted stomach. 'Er be a bit cackle-stomached'. The *cackle* part at first seems unusual, as it normally expresses bird noises or human laughter; but several dialects used it in the sense of 'chattering' or 'gabbling', which could easily describe a very noisy stomach, and thus the associated temperament.

cadgy (*adjective or adverb*)

Ireland, Northumberland, Scotland, Yorkshire

In good spirits, cheerful. The word appears in a variety of spellings, such as *cadgie*, *cagie*, and *kedgy*, and was very widely used in Scotland. From Ayrshire: 'The old man, cagie with the drink he had gotten, sang like a daft man'. In East Anglia it appears as *kedgy*. Its origin is unknown, but a verb of dynamic action, such as *catch*, could have had an influence.

cag-mag *or* **keg-meg** (*noun or verb*)

Cheshire, Devon, Gloucestershire, Kent, Lancashire, Lincolnshire, Norfolk, Northumberland, Nottinghamshire, Shropshire, Suffolk, Warwickshire, Worcestershire, Yorkshire

Chatter, gossip; grumble, quarrel; practical joke, mischief. This curious compound probably started out as a shortened form of *cackle*, which was then echoed with a nonsense second element, as in *super-duper*. People must have liked the sound of it, as it developed a remarkable range of senses and came to be used all over the country. Apart from the 'chattering' meanings, it was also used for tough meat, unwholesome food, loitering about, and simpletons. You really had to take note of the context to be sure you understood it correctly. From Devon: 'He's always up to some cag-mag or t'other' – that must be the 'mischief' sense. From Worcestershire: 'them two owd [old] critters upsta'rs a cagmaggin' like thaay allus [always] be' – that sounds like quarrelling. From Shropshire: 'I conna ate [can't eat] sich cag mag as that; it met [might] do fur a dog, but it inna fit for a Christian' – definitely bad meat.

camsteery (*adjective*)

Northumberland, Scotland, Sussex

Wild, unmanageable, obstinate. This is *cam* in the sense of 'bent from the straight', 'crooked' and *steer* meaning 'guide'. Horses are camsteery, but so are people. From Berwickshire: 'He had a wild, camstary pony'. From Perthshire: 'The'll aye be some camsteary craturs in the warld'. And from Fife, a truly remarkable coinage, presumably expressing a particularly forceful degree of camsteeriness: *camstroudgeous*.

cank (*adjective or noun*)

† Bedfordshire, Cheshire, Derbyshire, Lancashire,
Leicestershire, Northamptonshire, Nottinghamshire,
Shropshire, Staffordshire, Wales, Warwickshire,
Wiltshire, Worcestershire

Cank is one of those words that turns up all over the country with wildly diverse meanings, but often to do with chattering or gossiping. As with *cag-mag*, there must surely be a phonetic echo of *cackle* lying behind it. In Lancashire, a good place to chat in was called a *canking-pleck*. In some areas the word could also describe someone who made no noise at all ('dumb') or who was in a bad mood – though with such a meaning it could easily be showing the influence of *canker*. From Shropshire: 'I toud 'er a bit o' my mind, an' 'er 'uff'd an' ding'd an' went off in a fine cank'.

capadocious (*adjective*)

† Devon, Yorkshire

Splendid, excellent. From Devon: 'I tellee I've a-had a capadocious dinner'. It turns up as *capadosha* in Yorkshire. The origin is unclear: it sounds like a blend of *cap* (something that can't be surpassed, as in 'That caps everything') with an *-ous* ending (meaning 'full of', as in *ferocious*), but where the medial *d* comes from is a puzzle. There's an echo of *delicious* (and *Mary Poppins* – *supercallifragilisticexpialidocious*).

cataclue (*noun*)

Orkney and Shetland Isles

A number of people running in disorder and impeding each other. There is a link with cats, but not the one that immediately comes to mind. We need to know that *cat's clover* was used in this part of Scotland as one of the many folk names of *bird's-foot trefoil* – a flowering plant that rapidly spreads in all directions, like clover. Look at a field with bird's-foot trefoil all over it, and the association is easy to see.

cattie-bargle (*noun*)

Scotland

A noisy, angry quarrel among children, and among adults behaving in a childish way. *Cattie-wurrie* had a similar use. *Caterwaul* – from the wailing of cats on heat – is the word whose form comes closest in general colloquial English. In some dialects, such as Yorkshire, *caterwauling* described any man who went out courting at night, whether he howled or not.

caw-magging (*adjective*)

Northamptonshire

Idle, lazy, gaping. There was something about the sound of *caw* that made it often used to describe people in negative ways. The cry of rooks, crows, and other harsh-sounding birds has been applied to human talk in a contemptuous way since at least the sixteenth century, so it's hardly surprising to see it used for other aspects of behaviour. We find *cawney* in Berkshire for a very stupid person; *cawking* in Gloucestershire for someone who was awkward or gawky.

ceffle *(verb)*
Lancashire

To cough slightly and sharply; pronounced 'ke-full'. Given the many kinds of cough people are plagued with, it's strange that English hasn't developed a fuller vocabulary for the condition. *Ceffle* is an exception. There's a similar word in Dutch, where *keffen* means 'yelp' (like a fox or dog).

certy *(adjective)*
Somerset

Obstinate, self-willed; pronounced 'sir-ty'. 'She war so certy and positive like, there war no sayin' nothin' to 'er'. It's a shortened form of *certain*, and a natural development of meaning from its sense of 'resolved, determined'.

chaffering *(noun)*
Cornwall, Cumberland, Kent, Lancashire, Lincolnshire, London, Scotland, Westmorland, Yorkshire

Haggling over a bargain. From Lancashire: 'Don't waste no more time in chaffering'. Etymologically, it means 'sale' (*chap*, as in the old word for a merchant, *chapman*) and 'going' (as in *faring*). But its dialect sense must also have benefited from the unrelated word *chaffer*, meaning 'banter'. If you *chaff* someone, you're using provoking language, but in a light-hearted way.

chamble *or* chomble (*verb*)

Norfolk, Northamptonshire, Nottinghamshire, Shropshire, Suffolk, Warwickshire

To chew into small bits; gnaw, nibble. It's part of a family of *ch-* words all reflecting the action of chewing – such as the widely used *chaw*, as well as *chavel*, *chavver*, *chark*, *chiggle*, *chobble*, *champ* and *chomp*. From Warwickshire: 'I don't wonder at his being badly; he bolts his meat and never half chombles it'.

chang (*noun or verb*)

Cumberland, Lancashire, Scotland, Westmorland

A loud, confused noise; noisy gossip. An echoic word, reflecting sounds heard also in *clang* and *bang*. From Westmorland: 'Yah couldn't hear yer aansell speeak fer udder folkses chang'. It wasn't restricted to the human voice: musicians could make a chang; so could dogs.

cheeping-merry (*adjective*)

Lancashire

Half-drunk, elevated. Of the hundreds of words for being tipsy in English, this must surely be one of the happiest.

chice *or* jice (*noun*)

Essex, Norfolk, Suffolk

A small quantity or portion of anything. From Essex: 'Just a little chice more salt'. The same notion turns up in Ireland as *chi*: 'A chi of barach [barley]'. The etymology is unclear, but it may be a version of *chiche*, which came into English from French in the Middle Ages, with the meaning of 'sparing' or 'parsimonious'.

chilth (*noun*)

Cornwall

The chilliness of the atmosphere – presumably opposed to *warmth*. 'I cumd home early to avoid the chilth'. The *-th* ending, making nouns from verbs (as in *growth*) or adjectives (as in *truth*), is rare in English, but it nonetheless carries a certain appeal, as it's used in playful formations, such as *coolth*. There are other examples below (*dryth, feelth, sidth*).

chocketty (*adjective*)

Surrey

Of a bad cold: affecting the throat. The source is probably *choke*, a similar development being seen in *chock-full* – 'full to the point of choking'. But several dialects, especially in the West Country, called molar teeth *chock-teeth*, where *chock* here is a variant of *cheek* – the teeth closest to the cheeks. And *chock* was also used in some places to mean the flesh around the jaws – the chops. Whatever the source, *chocketty* must have been a useful addition to the very limited vocabulary English has for describing physical symptoms (see also *ceffle*) – as anyone knows who has tried to explain to a doctor exactly how they are feeling.

chollous (*adjective*)

Lincolnshire, Yorkshire

Of persons: harsh, stern, irritable. Of weather: cold, bleak. From Yorkshire: 'He's a nasty chollous sooat of a chap'. 'T'wind's varry chollous'. The applications of this word were diverse. Apples could also be chollous (sour), as could some medicines. And soil could be chollous (difficult to work), as could roads (with a poor surface). The source of all these is a familiar word: *churlish*.

chorp (*verb*)

Scotland

To emit a creaking sound. From Lothian: 'My shoon [shoes] are chorpin' – because of water getting into them. It's difficult to think of an echoic form that exactly reflects the sound made when walking in waterlogged footwear, but this isn't far off.

clabber (*noun*)

Cumberland, Ireland, Scotland

Soft, sticky mud. In Sidney Gilpin's *Songs and Ballads of Cumberland* (1866) there's a poem called 'The Raffles Merry Neet', in which a landlord gets into such a rage over the way his tavern has been treated that the merry-makers 'fain wad [would] ha' dabb'd him wi' clabber' – but don't dare to. It's originally a Gaelic word: *clabar*, 'mud'.

click-ma-doodle (*adjective or noun*)

Devon

A badly finished piece of work. 'A poor click-ma-doodle job'. This is *click* in the sense of something happening 'on and off' – heard also in *clicker* for a chronic invalid, whose illness is intermittent. It's reinforced by *doodle*, which turns up in various words expressing the idea of 'foolishness' (such as *fopdoodle* and *monkey-doodle*). And there's doubtless a link with *click-handed* for a left-handed person.

cloffin (*verb*)

Scotland

The act of sitting idle by the fire (just as an *ashiepattle* does – see above). The origin isn't clear, but there could be a link with a *cloff*, used in the North of England and Scotland to describe the fork of a tree (the *cleft*) where the branch joins (sits idly by?) the trunk.

cock-throppled (*adjective*)

Cumberland, Westmorland

Having a well-developed Adam's apple. *Thropple* was an old word for a throat or neck, and presumably the distinctive throat of a rooster motivated the comparison. In the Lakes area this was then applied figuratively when making a fence: if some branches were laid in to fill up a gap and some of them stuck upwards, the fence was said to be cock-throppled.

cogglety (*adjective*)

Ireland, Northumberland, Westmorland, Yorkshire

Shaky, unsteady. From Westmorland: a man makes a pile of stones, 'but they war varra coglety to clim ower'. *Coggle* was widely used in Scotland and the North of England to mean 'move unsteadily'. It's probably a word where the sound echoes the sense, like *jiggle* and *joggle*.

cognost (*verb*)

Scotland

To sit close together and plot some harmless mischief. 'Look at them two cognostin'. This is a rare example of a technical legal expression entering everyday conversation, but in an adapted sense. To *cognosce* in Scottish law was to carry out an investigation in order to reach a legal decision. The same Latin source turns up in *take cognizance of*.

condiddle *or* **kindiddle** (*verb*)

Cornwall, Devon, Scotland, Somerset

Entice, take away clandestinely. From Cornwall: 'You'm like Eve in the garden. She was kindiddled and did eat'. There is a link with the general colloquial use of *diddle*, 'cheat'. The source may be an Old English verb meaning 'deceive', but a playful origin (as with *doodle* and *doddle*) can't be ruled out.

confloption (*noun*)

Cornwall, Norfolk, Suffolk

Flurry, confusion. From Norfolk: 'I'm all in a confloption'. The source is probably *flap* rather than *flop* – as when one is *in a flap* – with the other elements added playfully, based on similar-sounding words, such as *confusion*.

coppish (*noun*)

Wales

The part of the trousers that buttons in front. From Glamorgan, a contributor soberly comments: 'In use among the lower orders at Merthyr Tydvil'. It is a linguistic memory of the *codpiece*, the appendage at the front of male hose or breeches, often referred to in sixteenth-century Elizabethan drama. In Shakespeare's *Love's Labour's Lost*, Berowne, newly fallen in love, calls Cupid the 'king of codpieces'.

corrosy (*noun*)

Cornwall, Devon

An old grudge handed down from father to son; an annoyance. It appears in a variety of spellings, but all reflect the source word, *corrosive*. From Cornwall: 'She'll never bear a coresy against anybody for long'.

craichy (*adjective*)

Cheshire, Derbyshire, Leicestershire, Lincolnshire, Nottinghamshire, Shropshire, Staffordshire, Warwickshire, Worcestershire

Of a person: ailing, shaky. Of a house: dilapidated. From Staffordshire: 'I thought he'd goo off this winter, he's bin very craichy for a good while'. From Shropshire: 'a terrible craitchy owd 'ouse'. It's an adaptation of *creaky*.

cramble *or* **crammle** (*verb*)

Cheshire, Cornwall, Cumberland, Derbyshire, Lancashire, Lincolnshire, Northumberland, Nottinghamshire, Staffordshire, Westmorland, Yorkshire

To walk with difficulty, hobble along stiffly. From Yorkshire: 'Poor awd man, he can hardly crammle'. It belongs with a group of words where the primary meaning was to do with pressing or squeezing, such as *cram*, *cramp*, and *crumple*, and it prompted a number of derived expressions. For instance, if you were walking as if with sore feet, you were going *cramble-toes*.

crimpledy (*adverb*)

Leicestershire, Lincolnshire, Northamptonshire, Worcestershire, Yorkshire

Totteringly, lamely. From Worcestershire: 'He noticed how crimpledy she walked'. The associated verb is to *crimple*, which meant 'hobble, limp' as well as 'wrinkle, shrivel up'. Clearly, there's an association with *crumple*, but the vowel quality makes a big difference. If you were to crumple a piece of paper, you would crush it without taking any particular care; but if you crimpled it, the implication is that you would be handling it with a certain amount of finesse. Probably a similar nuance distinguished walking *crimpledy* as opposed to *crumpledy* – you would be much more bent and unsteady if you were the latter.

cronk (*verb*)

Cumberland, Nottinghamshire, Westmorland, Yorkshire

Crouch, sit huddled up. From Yorkshire: 'Miners and colliers will cronk daan i' th' cabin for a taum [time], when they come aat o' th' pit'. It also had a less favourable meaning: 'lounge, sit about gossiping'. The *Penrith Observer* in 1897 was in no doubt: 'Cronkin' about a public house is a bad sign'.

crottle (*noun*)

Cumberland, Durham, Northumberland, Scotland, Westmorland, Yorkshire

Fragment, crumb. From Renfrewshire: 'Lay on twa-three crottils on the fire'. The word derives from *crot*, a Middle English word meaning 'particle, bit'. Earlier history is unclear, but it sounds like an echoic word, with *crittle* a variant form.

crumpsy (*adjective*)

Cheshire

Ill-tempered, cross. 'Yo bin very crumpsy this mornin'. There's an obvious phonetic echo of *grumpy*, and thus of *grunt*, which seems to be the source of this family of words. *Crump* was widely used across the North of England and into Scotland in the same sense. The *-sy* ending adds a tone of mocking contempt, as with *boundsy* (see above) and *tipsy*.

cumpuffled (*adjective*)

Northamptonshire

Confused, bewildered. 'I was so cumpuffled I didn't know what I was about'. Using *puff* to describe the way we can push out the cheeks to express frustration has been in English a long time, from at least the fifteenth century. The *cum* part is an adaptation of *com-*, a prefix often used to intensify a meaning – 'completely puffled'.

curglaff (*noun*)

Scotland

The shock felt in bathing at the first plunge into cold water – and thus also panic-struck. In a Banffshire poem, a man is described as 'Curgloft, confounded . . .' Several words beginning with *gl-* refer to something happening quickly, as in *glimpse*. In Scotland, a *gloff* was a sudden fright. It's here intensified by the use of *cur-*, a prefix from Gaelic meaning 'utterly'. We see it again in *kerfuffle*, 'disorder' – originally *curfuffle*.

cusnation *or* **cussnation** (*adjective or noun*)

Gloucestershire, Hampshire, Wiltshire

An expletive – a euphemistic blend of *cuss* ('curse') and *damnation*. From Wiltshire: 'Don't you be took in by that cusnation old rascal'.

D

daberlick (*noun*)

 Scotland

A mildly insulting way of talking about someone who is tall and skinny. From Banffshire: 'Here's that daberlick o' a chiel [child].' The word was also used for long stringy seaweed, for ragged clothing, and for hair that hangs down in tangled and separate locks. It could be a quite useful word these days, with torn jeans so fashionable.

daggy (*adjective*)

 Cumberland, Durham, Lancashire, Norfolk,
Northumberland, Scotland, Suffolk, Yorkshire

Wet, drizzly, misty. From Cumberland: 'The weather is turn'd monstrous daggy'. It's one of a group of words of similar meaning: *daggly*, *dagging*, *dagged*. They all come from *dag*, 'drizzle', which is related to *dew*. Variants were found all over the country.

danglements (*noun*)

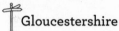 Yorkshire

The hanging appendages of a garment, fringes, tassels. 'She thought the ladies had too many danglements'. As with many uses of the verb *dangle*, there's a nuance of untidiness and disapproval.

darricky (*adjective*)

Gloucestershire

Rotten, decayed. Rotten timber, for example, would be described as *darricky*. The origin is unclear, but there's an echo of *rickety* here, which is an application to objects of the instability associated with the bone-weakness caused by *rickets*.

dateless (*adjective*)

Cheshire, Derbyshire, Lancashire, Lincolnshire, Westmorland, Yorkshire

Having the faculties failing through age or suffering. 'Mother is gone dateless wi' sorrow', says Sylvia in Chapter 28 of Mrs Gaskell's *Sylvia's Lovers* (1863). The word could also be used to describe someone unconscious, as from a blow. From Lancashire: 'They laid her upo' th' couch cheer [chair], as dateless as a stone'.

deceivery (*noun*)

Scotland

A habit or course of deceit. It's much more than describing a single instance of being deceitful. *Deceivery* captures the nuance that someone is a habitual deceiver. The -*ery* ending here, rather unusually, expresses 'a characteristic state of being', seen also in *knavery*. There's an old Renfrewshire rhyme: 'He's free o' deceivery, the basest o' knavery'.

deepooperit (*adjective*)

Scotland

Applied to someone in a state of imbecility, mentally or physically; worn out. 'A very common expression as applied to bodily frailty', says an observer from the Shetland Isles. Its potential usefulness extends well beyond those islands. I regularly feel deepooperit.

densh (*adjective*)

Cumberland, Durham, Northumberland, Yorkshire

Dainty, fastidious, squeamish. The etymology is unclear, but may be related to 'Danish': in Norfolk and Lincolnshire the hooded crow, which was thought to come from Denmark, was called a *denshman*. *Densh* was evidently used quite a lot in compounds, such as *densh-stomached* for someone with a fastidious taste or appetite. But my favourite derivation is the description of someone with an affected manner of speaking: *densh-gobbed.*

derrum (*noun*)
 Yorkshire

A deafening noise; a confusion of sounds. It's the associated description by one of Joseph Wright's dialect consultants that captures the imagination: it is like 'the rumbling, creaks, and cracks of an old mangle, together with the talk of several people who are putting it to use'.

dimracker (*noun*)
Worcestershire

A disaster; a complete failure. From the south-east of the county: 'If we gets no more rain this April than us did last, it'll be a dimracker o' they gooseberries'. It sounds like a popular phonetic adaptation of *disaster*.

discomfrontle (*verb*)
Norfolk, Northamptonshire, Suffolk

To disarrange, discompose. If you're discomfrontled, your normal state of mind or body has been seriously disturbed. It seems to be a blend of several negative feelings – *discomfit, affront,* or *confront,* with echoes of *discomfort* and *discomfortable.* You're definitely upset.

dixie-fixie (*noun*)

Scotland

A state of confinement, usually in prison. *Dixie* was a word meaning a sharp chiding. It probably comes from the time when Latin was spoken in schools, and a teacher would end an observation with *dixi* – 'I have said it' – meaning he wasn't prepared to tolerate any further response from his class. It would have been a short semantic step from here to a magistrate sending someone down.

doaty (*verb*)

Devon, Somerset

To nod the head when dozing in a sitting position. An Exmouth magazine in 1810 talks of someone 'doatee in the chimley coander' [in the chimney corner]. Anyone listening to an unexciting lecture would have no trouble seeing the modern relevance of this word.

docity *see* **odocity**

doggery-baw (*noun*)

Lincolnshire

Nonsense. 'Don't argle with him, he talks such doggery-baw'. *Doggery*, meaning 'doglike behaviour', has had a wide range of uses since at least the sixteenth century, with its earliest recorded usage meaning 'abusive language'. To 'speak doggery' was to be rude and insulting.

doppet (*verb*)

Gloucestershire

To play a musical instrument jerkily. As I write this, a lad has been doppeting on an amplified guitar in a house some distance away, on an otherwise peaceful Sunday afternoon. There might be an etymological link with *dope*, but I suspect his closer neighbours are thinking of a stronger word.

dottled (*adjective*)

Lincolnshire, Scotland

Said of anyone acting in a silly, foolish, or confused way. 'If I hadn't been so dottled I'd've thought of that!' The word was especially used to talk about someone apparently in a state of dotage. 'The poor chap's gone quite dottled.' A *dottle-trot* described an old man walking along in quick, short steps.

dowpy (*adjective*)

Northumberland

Of a pregnant woman: having a rounded shape. The origin lies in an Old Norse word for a rounded cavity which arrived in English during the Middle Ages as *doup*. Over the years it came to be used all over the North of England (and also in Scotland and Ireland) for a variety of shapes – the end of an egg, a burned-down candle, a nose, a person's posterior . . . and (perhaps most usefully, for it is a shape that lacks good descriptors) the pregnant form.

drang (*noun*)

Cornwall, Devon, Dorset, Gloucestershire, Hampshire, Isle of Wight, Somerset, Wales, Wiltshire

A narrow passage or lane between two walls, hedges, etc. The vowel varies greatly – sometimes *drong*, *dreng*, *dring*, *drung* – but in some form it was noted all over the West Country during the nineteenth century, along with *drangway*. It was sometimes also used for an open ditch or drain. In all cases, the common element is narrowness, and the notion of pressure – people passing through a narrow space – explains an etymological link with *throng*.

drowk (*verb*)

Huntingdonshire, Northamptonshire

Of plants: to wilt from want of water. The origin is unclear, though there's clearly an echo of *droop*. It was a favourite word of the poet John Clare: 'Drowking lies the meadow-sweet, / Flopping down beneath one's feet' (1820).

drunketting (*adjective*)

Berkshire

Given to getting drunk. 'Thee girt drunkettin' fool, come home with me direckly minnit [this minute]'. The nuance of predisposition differentiates it from other derivatives in this field, such as *drunkensome* and *drunky*, where the person is already (as they used to say in Lincolnshire) 'drunk as a boiled owl'.

dryth (*noun*)

Berkshire, Cornwall, Devon, Dorset, Gloucestershire, Hampshire, Isle of Wight, Kent, Pembrokeshire, Somerset, Surrey, Sussex

Dryness, drought, dry air. We have *warmth, coolth, length, depth, breadth* . . . so why not *dryth*? It was widely used across the South of England. From Sussex, a proverb: 'Drythe never yet bred dearth'. It even developed some extended meanings, such as 'thirst'. But it never caught on in standard English. Shame.

dumbfounder (*verb*)

Berkshire, Devon, Hampshire, Northamptonshire, Scotland, Sussex, Warwickshire, Yorkshire

Confuse, stupefy, stun. *Dumbfound* is such an expressive verb it's surprising the derivative forms didn't enter standard English. Examples from widely separated dialects suggest it was being used everywhere in Britain, along with an adverb, *dumbfounderedly*, two adjectives, *dumbfoundered* and *dumbfoundering*, and a noun, *dumbfounderment*.

dwam (*noun*)

Cornwall, Cumberland, Devon, Durham, Gloucestershire, Ireland, Lancashire, Northumberland, Scotland, Yorkshire

A swoon, faint, sudden feeling of faintness. The vowel is long, as shown by numerous variant spellings, such as *dwalm*, *dwarm*, and *dwaum*. From Lothian in 1895: 'Me gang to the kirk! No likely! The verra thocht o't brings a dwam ower me'. The word was mainly found throughout Scotland and the North of England, but it was also recorded in the English south-west, and in Ireland too. It generated a family of derived words – you might be troubled with *dwaminess* or feel *dwamish* or *dwamy*.

E

eardly (*adjective or adverb*)

Lincolnshire

Very, exceedingly. Spellings include *eadly*, *eadily*, *heedly*, and *yeardly*. Its various uses are all to do with increased size or strength. 'A great eardly tonup [turnip]' – unusually large. 'He preaches eadily' – forcefully. The source is an Old English word *heardlice*, which developed into *hardly* – but in its original sense of 'vigorously' (long before it weakened to mean 'barely').

eptish *see* **aptish**

ernful (*adjective or adverb*)

Kent, Sussex

Sad, lamentable, sorrowful. From Kent: 'ernful tunes', 'ernful sick'. There's clearly a link to *yearn*, earlier spelled *yern*, which had an adjective form *yernful* that was still being used in the nineteenth century. Expressions such as *my yernful heart* would easily transmute into *my ernful heart*.

F

fainty (*adjective*)

Cheshire, Devon, Gloucestershire, Herefordshire, Oxfordshire, Scotland, Warwickshire, Worcestershire, Yorkshire

Of the weather: close, sultry, oppressive. From Devon: 'the weather is cruel fainty today'. This is evidently weather that is so sultry it makes you feel faint, and indeed, *fainty* was also widely used throughout the country to mean 'faint, weak'. Its earliest recorded use is actually by Bible translator William Tyndale, who talks of faith being 'feble and fayntye', and later literary users include Dryden and Coleridge. But the extension to the weather seems dialectal.

fandandering (*adjective*)

Northumberland

Idle, good-for-nothing. 'A fandanderin' body – nowther gentry nor common fowk – never did a hand's turn that I mind, and never did ill owther'. An Irish variant was *fandangling*. The etymology isn't clear, but it probably relates to *fandangle*, 'fantastic ornaments', which also developed the sense of 'nonsense', and that in turn may have come from the dance *fandango*, which became very popular in the eighteenth century.

fanty-sheeny (*adjective*)

 Devon

Showy, fanciful, over-particular. 'Dawntee let me zee no more ov yer fanty-sheeny ways'. The source is Italian *fantoccini*, describing puppets that moved using concealed strings. Fantoccini shows were popular in the eighteenth and nineteenth centuries, and are mentioned by Boswell, Hazlitt, Dickens, and others. Several toured throughout the West Country, so the extended sense may well have been known in Cornwall and Somerset too.

fawnicate (*verb*)

Kent, Sussex

To fondle affectionately. From Kent, a mother to her child when cuddling up to her: 'Bless you, you little fawnicating thing'. The source is *fawn*, 'showing fondness', as in standard English, but the verb with the *-icate* ending never became standard – presumably because it would have sounded too much like *fornicate* in upper-class pronunciation, where the *r* wasn't pronounced after a vowel. Dialects would have kept the *r* and avoided any confusion.

feelth (*noun*)

Leicestershire, Northamptonshire, Rutland, Warwickshire, Worcestershire

Feeling, sensation. A word, like *coolth*, that shows how the *-th* ending for nouns was once much more widely used than it is today. From Leicestershire: 'His feet is mortified, an' hasn't got no feelth in 'em'. Judging by the distribution, it was a useful word across a broad swathe of middle England.

fendy (*adjective*)

Cumberland, Durham, Lancashire, Northumberland, Scotland, Yorkshire

Clever, resourceful, good at managing, thrifty. From Yorkshire: 'He's a rare fendy little chap, he's always ather fishin' or mendin' his net'. The origin is the verb *defend*. Evidently, up north, if you're good at defending yourself, you're likely to be resourceful in other ways.

ferrick *or* ferruck (*verb or noun*)

Berkshire, Northamptonshire, Oxfordshire, Warwickshire

To fidget or move about restlessly. From Warwickshire: 'to ferruck about a house dusting corners'. And from Berkshire, a noun: 'I be all in a ferrick'. There are several related senses, such as 'scratch', all involving rapid or jerky movement. The word is a pronunciation variant of *ferret*, which has had some use in colloquial standard English such as when people are rummaging through drawers looking for something. When people visit Hay-on-Wye, which has lots of bookshops, they go ferret-ing – but I like the sound of *ferricking* better.

finnying (*adjective*)
† Suffolk

Timid, fearful. From the east of the county: 'She's that finnying she won't go out after dark'. The related expression 'No finny!' means 'No fear!' There's a possible connection with the supernatural beings known as *Finns*. Up in the Shetland Islands there was a long tradition, coming from Norway, of attributing magic powers to the Finns, who were said to be able to assume the form of amphibious animals, such as seals. One didn't mess with the Finns. The word may well have spread in Anglo-Saxon times, when the Danes were numerous in eastern England, and developed its wider meaning.

flapsy (*adjective*)
† Bedfordshire

Lazy, clownish; ill-bred, ill-natured. In the 1770s, someone is described as 'a great flapsy fellow'. Any impudent person might be called a *flapse*, and if you flapsed someone you were being cheeky. The word was also used to mean 'flabby', which is itself a modification of earlier *flappy*. That's probably where the meanings began: a general notion of 'flabbiness' led to an associated sense of 'laziness' and then to the somewhat less associated (but presumably often encountered) sense of 'crabbiness'.

flaup (*verb or noun*)
Westmorland, Yorkshire

To strike with something flexible – the *au* pronounced as in *flaw*. From Yorkshire: 'They've a set day at Darfield flee catchin, an a bit a rare good fun it is, for there they are wi their henkichers an dusters flaupin em dahn'. It's probably an adaptation of *flap*, but it came to be used in quite a wide range of contexts. You could *flaup down* in a chair wearily. An awkward-looking hat or cap would be described as *flauping*. And if you wanted to tell someone off gently, you could give them a good *flaup* across the head or shoulders with something soft, such as a towel or a rolled-up newspaper.

flerk (*noun or verb*)
Berkshire, Hampshire, London, Wiltshire

To jerk about, flourish; to flip or flap anything about. From London: 'Don't keep flerking that in my face'. Clearly a useful word to capture that intermediate state between flicking and jerking – and also used for doing anything hastily and inefficiently. From Hampshire: 'Just gie it a flerk over'.

flimp (*adjective*)

🜊 Gloucestershire, Leicestershire, Nottinghamshire, Suffolk, Warwickshire, Worcestershire

Limp, flabby. The blending of these two words was used to describe linen and clothing. A collar might be described as flimp if it lost its stiffness. In Worcestershire the blend was *limp* + *flimsy*: soft or delicate cloth was *flimslimp*.

flob *or* flub (*noun or verb*)

🜊 Oxfordshire, Scotland, Yorkshire

To puff, cause to swell up. Yeast added to flour would cause dough to *flob*. Clouds swollen with rain would be described as *flobby*. A swollen arm would be *flobbed up*. And it was a bluff put-down for inflated speech. From Yorkshire: 'Tha's all flob'. Also from Yorkshire: 'I can make a bigger flob on my cheeks than thou can on thine'. This application of the word travelled: in Dorset and Wiltshire a popular term of abuse was *flobberchops*. And in 2010 someone added this to the Urban Dictionary, with the meaning 'having chubby cheeks'. Dialect lives – online.

flunter (*noun*)

🜊 Cheshire, Lancashire, Yorkshire

A bit of rubbish, a state of confusion, an angry state of mind. This was a really popular word, widely used across the North of England. 'He wur eh sitch a flunter', writes Lancastrian Tom Bobbin in 1740. From Yorkshire: 'His loom is badly eawt o' flunter' – out of order. If your hair was 'all afflunters' it would be in a terrible state. Another Lancastrian recommends having a *flunter-drawer* for odds and ends. I used to have one, for linguistic miscellanea, but it got too small. It's a flunter room now. And that present-day usage reminds me that there's no predicting the future of a word. In fact, in 2007, someone in north-east Iowa started a blog and decided to call it *aflunters*. 'We all start out aflunters when we get out of bed in the morning', the blogger begins.

footer-footer (*verb*)

 Scotland

To walk in an affected, mincing manner. From Fife: 'I like to see a man plant his feet firmly on the ground and no gang footer-footerin' like a peacock wi' its tail spread'. No further comment needed, really.

forethink *or* forthink (*verb*)

Cheshire, Lancashire, Scotland, Yorkshire

To consider beforehand; or, to regret afterwards. From North Yorkshire, about an event that had received little preparation: 'There was nought foorethowten about'. If you were *forethinking*, you were being prudent. From Lancashire: 'It made me rayther for-think ever settin' eawt

[out]'. This group of words was widely used in earlier centuries, but only *forethought* – in the sense of anticipation, rather than regret – has survived in standard English.

frab (*verb*)

Cheshire, Cumberland, Derbyshire, Lancashire, Westmorland, Yorkshire

To struggle, argue; worry, fidget; irritate, excite. From Cheshire: 'You can frab a horse by pulling too hard at the reins'. The word seems to be a sound blend of *fret* and *crab*, or something similar, and the wide range of meanings suggests that it was very widely used, along with its derivatives. A baby teething? *Frabby*. Get out of bed on the wrong side? *Frabbly*. Irritated at someone? *Frabbit*.

frack (*verb*)

Gloucestershire, Norfolk, Northamptonshire, Suffolk

No, not the sense that makes the news these days. This verb turns up in various locations in such senses as 'abound, crowd together, fill to excess'. From Northamptonshire: 'The currant trees were as full as they could frack'. From East Anglia: 'The church was fracking full'. So anything full to overflowing would be *frackfull*. In Gloucestershire if you were *fracking* you were fussing about.

fribble (*verb*)

Cheshire, Norfolk, Scotland, Suffolk, Warwickshire, Yorkshire

To trifle, idle, fuss. From Suffolk: 'He goes fribbling about the whole day'. The word is a sound blend, probably from *frivolous* with the *-bble* ending used in words expressing repeated erratic movement (*wobble, dribble* . . .). I wasn't expecting to find a linguistic sense – 'to speak fine English' – but there was one in Norfolk. In response to a teacher explaining that 'grammar is the art of speaking and writing correctly', a student replied: 'Ow, miss, kinder what fooks in our part call framin or fribblin'.

frowsty (*adjective*)

Berkshire, Cheshire, Gloucestershire, Leicestershire, Northamptonshire, Nottinghamshire, Oxfordshire, Shropshire, Warwickshire, Wiltshire, Worcestershire

Musty, ill-smelling, not fresh; heavy-looking, peevish. It's echoed in several other words (*frown, frosty, crusty*), but is probably closest to *froward* (= 'from' + 'ward') – going contrary to a desired state of affairs. From Worcestershire: 'The snuff was frowsty'. From Shropshire: 'W'y yo' looken as sleepy an' frousty this mornin' as if yo' 'adna bin i' bed las' night'. Words with a similar sound and meaning – *frowsy* or *frowy* – have been recorded in most parts of the British Isles.

fubsy (*adjective*)

Lancashire, Yorkshire

Plump, in a nice sort of way. Rudyard Kipling liked this word. In *Jungle Book*, Baloo uses it in one of his laws of the jungle:

> 'Oppress not the cubs of the stranger, but hail them
>   as Sister and Brother,
> For though they are little and fubsy, it may be the
>   Bear is their mother.'

When in 2008 a dictionary company announced a list of words it would omit from its next edition, *The Times* led a 'save a word' campaign, with *fubsy* supported by, among others, Stephen Fry.

fummasing *or* **thumbasing** (*noun or verb*)

Cheshire, Lancashire

Fumbling with the hands as if the fingers were all thumbs. From Cheshire: 'What art fummasin with at th'lock?' The source is *thumb*, with the replacement of *th* by *f* – showing that this sound change isn't solely a modern ('Estuary English') phenomenon. The word would also be used if you were just dawdling. From Lancashire: 'Roger kept telling hur as he seed hur fummashin abeawt that hoo'd be too late'.

funch (*verb*)

Dorset, Hampshire, Isle of Wight

Push, thrust, strike with the fist. From the Isle of Wight: 'Don't keep a funchen me zo'. As a punch usually involves the fist anyway, it's likely that *funch* was used for less aggressive blows.

G

gadwaddick (*verb*)

 Norfolk

To jaunt, go on a pleasure trip. 'They do stare, these Broadland children, although the novelty of yachtin' and other folk gadwaddickin' on the Broads is wearing off'. In Worcestershire, *wadgiking* was to walk about in an awkward manner. The etymology isn't entirely clear. *Gad* is a common variant of *go* (as in *gad about*), but the *wad* element is obscure. It might be related to *wade*.

gangagous (*adjective*)

Devon

Careful, mindful – prononced gang-<u>gay</u>-juss. The word is an adaptation of *gang*, 'go'. 'I've bin moore gangag'ous o' my mouth than I hev o' religion', said a man who stayed at home from church to eat fruit.

gashly (*adjective*)

 Cornwall, Devon, Leicestershire, Suffolk, Sussex, Warwickshire, Wiltshire, Worcestershire

Terrible, dismal, hideous. An adaptation of *ghastly*. From Sussex: 'It be a gashly sight'. But it had a more general intensifying sense, much as we might say something was 'awful'. In Cornwall, a man was said to have 'a gashly temper'. In Wiltshire, a hedge was described as 'gashly high'. It had a modern reincarnation in Edward Gorey's macabre alphabet book, *The Gashlycrumb Tinies* (1963): 'A is for Amy who fell down the stairs . . . B is for Basil assaulted by bears . . .'

gazooly *or* **gazol** (*verb*)

 Cornwall

To be constantly uttering laments. A man who was very depressed admitted to 'gazoling all day long'. Another talked about the way he was 'gazoolying'. The origin seems to be the French verb *gazouiller*, 'warble' – as when a young bird is learning to sing.

giddling (*adjective*)

 Northamptonshire, Oxfordshire, Staffordshire, Warwickshire, Worcestershire

Unsteady, unreliable, thoughtless, rickety. An adaptation of *giddy*, applied to both people and objects. From

Staffordshire: 'I wonder at him fulin' wi' such a giddlin' wench like her'. From Worcestershire: 'Dunna yu get into that thahr boat. 'Tis a giddling thing, an' you'll sure to be drownded'.

glack (*noun or verb*)

 Scotland

Handful, morsel. From Aberdeenshire: a woman 'taks frae her pouch a glack of bread and cheese'. *Glac* was Gaelic for a narrow valley, or glen. Any V-like shape might then be called a glack, such as the fork of a tree, a fork in a road, the angle between the thumb and the forefinger, or the hollow of a hand when it was cupped to hold something. If I *glacked your mitten*, I would be giving you a tip – or a bribe.

glat (*noun*)

Gloucestershire, Herefordshire, Shropshire, Wales, Westmorland, Worcestershire

A gap in a hedge – or in your mouth, through loss of teeth. From Worcestershire: 'He's met him a-tryin' to git through a glat i' the hedge'. From Shropshire, a snippet of dialogue: 'I thought yo' wun gwein [going] to marry the cook at the paas'n's [parson's].' 'Aye, but 'er'd gotten too many glats i' the mouth fur me.'

glorys (*noun*)

Westmorland, Yorkshire

The eyes. From Yorkshire: 'My word, but he did oppen his glorys when he gate that bill'. It's a development of *glore*, 'stare, gaze fixedly', which has links with *glower* and *glare*. *Gloorers* was an old word for spectacles.

glox (*verb*)

Hampshire, Wiltshire

Of liquids: to make a gurgling sound when shaken inside a vessel. From Wiltshire: 'Fill the barrel full, John, or else it will glox in carriage'. In Scotland and parts of the North of England, the word appears as *glock* or *gluck*.

gnang *see* nang

goddle-house (*noun*)

Warwickshire

A house that has been vacant a long time and needs repair. 'Wonder when the Squire'll let that goddle house'. *Goddle* is probably derived from 'God will' – the future of the place is thought of as being in the hands of God. The label was never applied to an ordinary empty house. It had to be one that was on the verge of becoming a ruin.

granch *or* **graunch** (*verb*)

Cheshire, Derbyshire, Gloucestershire, Lancashire, Leicestershire, Nottinghamshire, Shropshire, Warwickshire, Worcestershire, Yorkshire

To crunch between the teeth, grind the teeth, eat noisily – a sound blend of such words as *grind* and *crunch*. From Warwickshire: 'I used to granch up all the crusteses'. The word was also used to describe the noise joints make when they crack, and to any scrunching sound. From Leicestershire: 'I heard the ice graunching under the wheels of the carriage'.

grob (*verb*)

Durham, Lincolnshire, Yorkshire

To search by the sense of feeling, as with the hand in any dark place. From Yorkshire: 'she's grobbing in her pocket an' can fin nowt'. It's a variant of *grope*, but the short vowel and the final *-b* convey a rougher, earthier, more active nuance. We see the same sort of energy in the way the word was also used to describe children playfully digging in soil or mud – *grobbing about*. And the idea of doing it over and over is there in a related verb, *grobble*.

grumptious (*adjective*)

Yorkshire

Inclined to grumbling, irritable, sullen. Quite a few old dialect adjectives derive from *grumble*, such as *grumly*, *grumphy*, *grumply*, and the simple *grum* – clearly related to *grim*. *Grumpy* was the form that entered standard colloquial English. It lacks the nuance of *grumptious* which – like *cautious*, *ambitious*, *superstitious*, and others – has a word-ending that expresses the notion 'full of' or 'characteristic of'. Any of us can be grumpy at times; but *grumptious* better describes someone for whom grumpiness is a character trait.

grut (*noun*)

Norfolk

Used in the phrase *to leave a swede in the grut*: to let alone, to leave a story untold. 'Lave that swede in the grut. That yarn's gettin' very near as old as your grandfather'. *Grut*, or *groot*, was 'mud, spoil, earth'. It's related to *grit*.

gruttling (*noun*)

Norfolk, Suffolk

A strange, inexplicable noise. From Norfolk: 'I hear a gruttling in the chimbly [chimney]'. It's probably a blend of such words as *grunt* and *rattling*. A Suffolk commentator thought it was like the noise of someone being throttled.

gurly (*adjective*)

Gloucestershire, Herefordshire, Ireland,
Northumberland, Scotland, Somerset

Said of weather, when it's rough, stormy, cold, or bleak.
From Lothian: 'There's a strang gurly blast, blawin' snell
[sharply] frae the north'. The word is a variant of *growl*,
or a representation of the sound of growling, which in
Scotland was often *gurr*. *Gurly* was also used for snarling
dogs, gnarled trees, and surly people.

H

hagg (*noun*)

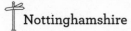
Nottinghamshire

A hole in a road. 'Tek some stones an' fill up that hag i' th' road'. A road with many haggs would be *haggy*. On the moors, it would be a piece of soft bog. It's related to other Germanic words with senses to do with cutting or breaking, such as *hew* and *hack*. Applied to people, *hagged* or *haggit* meant 'worn out, tired, harassed'.

hainish *or* **ainish** (*adjective*)

Essex, Hertfordshire

Unpleasant, especially of the weather; also, awkward, ill-tempered. From Hertfordshire: 'He was such an ainish old man'. It's probably a local adaptation of *heinous*.

harriage (*noun*)

Devon, Norfolk, Northamptonshire, Suffolk,
Wiltshire

A disturbance, bustle, fuss; confusion, disorder. Spelling

varies greatly, reflecting pronunciations with both *r* and *l*. From Wiltshire: 'What a hallege!' – what a row! In parts of Suffolk, the nearby port led to a local adaptation, *go to Harwich*, meaning 'go to rack and ruin'. The word probably comes from a French loanword in Middle English, *orageux*, 'stormy'.

hask (*adjective*)

Cheshire, Cumberland, Derbyshire, Ireland, Lancashire, Lincolnshire, Scotland, Staffordshire, Warwickshire, Yorkshire

Of weather: dry, parching, or piercingly cold; also, rough to the touch; bitter to the taste. This was one of the most widely used dialect words in the British Isles, turning up in a variety of forms, such as *harsk*, *aske*, and *yask*. The common origin seems to be *harsk*, pronounced *hask* in the north, which eventually became *harsh* in standard English. People would talk about 'a hask wind' or a cow with 'a hask hide'; sour plums would be 'very hask', as would sugarless tea (to someone who takes sugar).

havage *or* haveage (*noun*)

Cornwall, Devon

Race, lineage, family stock. From Devon: 'Her come vrom a good haveage – the very daps [likeness] of her mother'. Someone from a family of ill repute would be said to be 'o' bad havage'. The source is the verb *have*, in its sense of 'come into possession of'.

havey-cavey (*adjective*)

Cumberland, Derbyshire, Lancashire, Lincolnshire, Northamptonshire, Nottinghamshire, Yorkshire

Unsteady, uncertain, doubtful, all in confusion. From Yorkshire: 'It was havey-cavey whether I came or not', 'Mi heead's all eyvy-keyvy this mornin'. The formation is like *higgledy-piggledy* and other reduplicating compounds, and is recorded in a wide range of pronunciations and spellings, such as *heevy-skeevy* (in Cumberland) and *heavely-keavely* (in Derbyshire). In Lincolnshire, if you were *on the havey-quavey* you were making inquiries or checking up on something.

heigh-go-mad (*adverb*)

Derbyshire, Lancashire, Yorkshire

Wildly, furiously, with great force – the first part often spelled *hei* or *hey*. From Yorkshire: 'Sum [factories] we chimleys on em, an't smook putherin at tops like heigo-mad'. From Lancashire: 'The horse broke the traces and ran off like heygomad'.

hengments (*noun*)

Yorkshire

Odds and ends, bric-a-brac, especially things hanging on a wall. 'I talked a bit t'maister about t'pictures and t'little hengments 'at wor heer an' theer'. In the singular form *hangment*, it had a totally different meaning. *What the hangment!* was an oath, widely used across the North and Midlands, derived from *hanging* in its sense of execution (in the same way as *hang it all!* is still said today).

hettle (*verb*)

Durham, Northumberland, Scotland, Yorkshire

To act in haste or anger. From Northumberland, a pitman, charged with throwing his lamp down the pit-shaft, said in his defence: 'He nobbut hettled it away an' it stotted off the flat sheets an' ganned doon the shaft'. If you were *hettle-tongued*, you were foul-mouthed. The word comes from Old English *hatol* – 'full of hatred'.

hocksy (*adjective*)

Berkshire, Gloucestershire, Oxfordshire, Wiltshire

Dirty, muddy, miry, soft, sticky – often spelled *hoxey*, *hoxy*, or *oxy*. It seems to refer to any ground into which the feet sink. From Wiltshire: 'It's about two miles in vine weather; but when it's hocksey, like this, we allows a mile for slippin' back'. The word is probably related to *hock*, referring to part of a leg. In this area, and also further north, to *hock* meant 'trample earth into a muddy condition', and thus to cause a mess as a result. From the West Midlands: 'Don't come a oxing over these stones what I've jest cleaned with them dirty shoes o' yorn'.

huckmuck (*adjective or noun*)

Berkshire, Devon, Dorset, Hampshire, Wiltshire

Confusion caused by all things being out of place, a muddle. From Devon: 'I nuver did zee sich a huck-muck place in awl my born days'. Further north, the same meaning was expressed by *huckermucker*. It was also one of the senses of *hugger-mugger*, used throughout England and Scotland – and made famous in its sense of 'secrecy' by Shakespeare in *Hamlet*, when King Claudius describes how ineptly he has handled the death of Polonius: 'we have done but greenly / In hugger-mugger to inter him'.

hummy (*adjective*)

Wales

Musty, going bad with damp. From Pembrokeshire: 'The bacon is gone hummy'. 'This pan smells hummy'. The source is *hum*, in its sense of 'smell disagreeably', which presumably arose from the low murmuring noise made by flies and other insects attracted to rotting food.

I

illify (*verb*)

Cumberland, Lancashire, Lincolnshire, Staffordshire, Westmorland, Yorkshire

To slander. From Yorkshire: 'Thare they ar, illifyin' an' backbitin ivery boddy'. It's an adaptation of standard English *vilify*, from *vile*. A small family of related words emerged: an *illifier* was a slanderer; and if you were *illified* you were, in an extension of the meaning, scandalized.

ireful (*adjective*)

Yorkshire

Angry, stormy, inflamed. A wound was said to 'look varry ireful', as were dark gathering clouds. *Ire*, from Latin *ira* 'anger', became poetic in standard English, but remained an everyday word in several dialects.

izzard (*noun*)

Cheshire, Cumberland, Derbyshire, Durham, Gloucestershire, Lancashire, Lincolnshire,

Northamptonshire, Northumberland, Scotland,
Suffolk, Wiltshire, Yorkshire

An old name for the letter *z*. It was widely used in dialects, and travelled to Virginia, where 'from A to izzard' is recorded with the meaning 'from beginning to end'. British developments included *izzardly*, 'to the last degree'. From Gloucestershire: 'The bull frightened him most izedly'. If you were 'as crooked as an izzard' you had a perverse disposition.

J

jammock *or* **jammuck** (*verb*)

Herefordshire, Norfolk, Shropshire, Suffolk

To squeeze, press, crush – a derivative of *jam* in its sense of 'press tightly'. Animals – and sometimes humans – who were *jammocked* were 'worn out, exhausted'. From Norfolk, of a donkey purchased for little money on account of an injury: 'it was not so malahacked [disabled] as to be jammucked for all that'.

janjansy (*adjective or noun*)

Cornwall

A two-faced person. Someone would be called 'a janjansy' or have 'a janjansy look'. The word is an adaptation of *Janus*, the Roman deity who guarded doors and gates, who was represented with two faces – one on the front and one on the back of his head.

jawbation (*noun*)

Hampshire, Huntingdonshire, Lincolnshire, Norfolk, Northamptonshire, Northumberland, Oxfordshire, Somerset, Sussex, Warwickshire, Yorkshire

A long and tedious harangue; a scolding, severe lecture, or reprimand. From Lincolnshire: 'She nearly drove me scranny [crazy] with her jawbation'. In Yorkshire, and probably elsewhere, such a person was described as *jawbacious*: 'loquacious'.

jawmotry (*noun*)

Lincolnshire, Yorkshire

Used especially in the phrase *out of jawmotry*, 'out of shape or order'. In the plural, it was used to describe objects that were in shreds. From North Yorkshire, describing a garment hanging in rags in the wind: 'It's all hung i' jawmatrees'. The spelling hides the unexpected origin: *geometry*.

jice *see* **chice**

jobbernowl (*noun*)

Devon, Lancashire, Lincolnshire, Scotland, Suffolk, Yorkshire

A dunce, dolt, blockhead. From Yorkshire: 'This is no work for a jobbernowl'. The second part of the word is well-known: a *noll* is an old Anglo-Saxon word for a head. But whence *jobber*? It may have developed from a French word, *jobard*, 'fool', that came into English in the Middle Ages. That in turn seems to have come from the Biblical character Job, who was accused of being a fool by his family and friends. A small family of related words developed. If you were *jobberheaded* you were stupid. If you were a chatterbox, a nonsense-talker, you were a *jobbernowt*.

jounce (*verb*)

Essex, Norfolk, Suffolk

In gardening: to rake very fine. 'I've jounced that flower border all over'. The word could also mean 'to rock a child or cradle, as in, 'She jounced the babe on her knee', and this suggests a phonetic source, as it echoes other words with a meaning of sudden movement, such as *bounce*, *flounce*, *pounce*, and *trounce*.

jubbity (*noun*)

Yorkshire

A difficulty, vexatious occurrence, misfortune. 'He's had some jubbities in his lifetime'. The spelling hides the relationship with standard English *jeopardy*. Trouble in general was *jubberment*, and sometimes *jubblement*.

jurgy (*adjective*)

Shropshire

Contentious, inclined to pick a quarrel. 'The agent wuz mighty jurgy, I 'ad t' mind whad I said to 'im'. The origin is unclear, but there was a Latin word, *jurgium*, meaning a brawl or contention, which might be connected. On the other hand, similar sounding words with similar meaning also exist, such as *jar*, so the source might lie there.

K

kazzardly (*adjective*)

Cheshire, Lancashire, Shropshire, Yorkshire

Precarious, risky, uncertain. From Lancashire: 'It's a kazzardly onsartin loife we lead'. The word was often applied to the weather: kazzardly weather was changeable and unsettled. Weak or sickly animals were also described as kazzardly. It's probably a local pronunciation of *hazardly*, which is recorded in the sixteenth century.

keffel (*noun*)

Herefordshire, Scotland, Shropshire, Somerset, Warwickshire, Worcestershire, Yorkshire

An old or inferior horse; a big clumsy man or beast; anything of inferior quality. From Warwickshire: 'Mind where yer treadin', yer great keffel'. The word seems to have spread north and south from the counties bordering Wales, for the origin is certainly Welsh *ceffyl*, 'horse'. It came to be widely used throughout the North Country.

keg-meg *see* **cag-mag**

kenspeck *or* **kenspeckle** (*adjective*)

Cumberland, Durham, Ireland, Lancashire,
Lincolnshire, Northumberland, Scotland, Shropshire,
Westmorland, Yorkshire

Conspicuous, remarkable, easily distinguishable or recognizable. The word appears in a variety of spellings, such
as *kenspak*, *kentsback*, and *kinseback*. From Yorkshire: 'As
kenspak as a cock on a church-broach [spire]'. The first
element is probably the same as *ken*, 'know' (as in Scots
'Do you ken?'). It's also seen in *kensmark* – a peculiar
mark or spot by which anything may be easily recognized
– also used across the North of England.

kindiddle *see* **condiddle**

knivy (*adjective*)

Staffordshire

Penurious, miserly, careful to the point of meanness.
'Her's too knivy to gie 'em enough to ate'. And if you
really wanted to emphasize the point, as in this remark
about a recently deceased individual, there was a derived
form, *knivetious*: 'We allays said he was knivetious, but
we dain't expect he'd leave soo much'. Presumably the
word began as an extension of a 'cutting down' sense of
knife.

kobnoggle (*verb*)

Lancashire

To pull the hair and then hit the head with the knuckles. From a combination of *cob* 'head' and *knock* or *nobble*. Evidently an ancient Lancastrian rite of passage.

kysty (*adjective*)

Cumberland, Lancashire, Westmorland, Yorkshire

Dainty, fastidious, difficult to please. From Cumberland, said to a child who was being fussy about his meal: 'Thu lyle kysty fairy' – you little unthankful imp. The word was also spelled *coysty* in Yorkshire, which suggests a link with being *coy*.

L

lab-dab (*noun*)
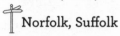
Norfolk, Suffolk

A profuse perspiration. 'The wench is all of a lab dab'. *Labber* was a widely used word for activities associated with water. From Tyneside: 'splashing and labbering about i' the tide'. Muddy roads would be *labbery*, as would rainy weather. Treacle was called *labber-gob* in Yorkshire because of the mess it made on your mouth. There are clear phonetic links with *dab* and *dabble*, and also with *lap*. In Essex the word turns up as *lap-dab*.

lally-wow (*noun*)
Lincolnshire

A cat. 'The lally-wow is kittling'. The second part echoes the cat's sound, as so many similar words do, such as *mew*, *mewl*, and (common in Middle English) *wrawe* and *wrawl*. The first part is not so clear. It may be an adaptation of babytalk *la-la* or *lulla*, used to infants and animals, and which gave rise to the verb *lall* and the noun *lullaby* in standard English. Or it may be a version of *caterwaul*.

larmy (*adjective*)

Somerset

Sorrowful. From French *larmeux*, 'full of tears' – a borrowing that somehow reached Somerset but didn't enter the standard language. The nearest we get is the old architectural term *larmier*, referring to the coping on a wall that serves to throw off the (drops, 'tears' of) rain.

lassified (*adjective*)

Yorkshire

Young-looking. Said of women, *lassie* being a widely used word for a young woman or little girl in Scotland and the North Country. 'E passed t'remark 'at [that] ye were a bit lassified'. We might expect *laddified* to be the male equivalent, but it was never recorded.

leary *or* **leery** (*adjective*)

Cornwall, Devon, Dorset, Hampshire, Somerset, Sussex

Hungry, empty, faint and exhausted from hunger. From Dorset: 'I am that leery I can feel my stomach rubbing against my backbone'. From Somerset: 'I was that leery, I was fir t'eat a raw turmut [turnip]'. The word was also widely used across the South of England without the *-y* ending in the same sense. From Worcestershire: 'I feels mighty leer, I mun 'ave a bit of nuncheon'. Further north, it had the more general meaning of something being 'empty' or 'unladen'. *Leary* crossed the Atlantic too, and is recorded in some American dialect dictionaries. It all started in Old English, where the word for 'emptiness' was *lærnes*. And 'empty' is *leer* in German and *laar* in Dutch.

lennock (*adjective*)

Cornwall, Devon, Dorset, Hampshire, Somerset, Sussex, Yorkshire

Limp, flabby; pliant, flexible; pendulous. A word that had a wide range of applications. People, parts of the body, buildings, parts of buildings, plants, even corpses could all be described as *lennock* or *lennucky*. From Yorkshire: 'Leavin' this stick o' rhubub aht t'door all t'neet hes made it lennucky'. There's probably a historical link with *long* and *length*.

lerry *or* lirry (*noun*)

Hertfordshire, Lincolnshire

A whim, fancy, caprice; a pretext, trick, fib. From Lincolnshire: 'He's full of his lerries'. In the Isle of Wight, it turns up as *lurry*, meaning 'loose talk', and spellings from other locations around the South of England show the other two vowels – *larry* and *lorry*. The word's source is probably the most scholarly in this book. It's a shortening of *liriripe* or *liripoop*, which describes the long tail of a graduate's hood. The meaning then shifted to what someone would say or do: you would *know your liripoop* – know your part. It would have been only a short step from there for ordinary folk to abbreviate the word to describe scholarly speech they felt to be obscure or evasive, and then to use it for anyone putting on airs or trying to hide the truth.

lewth (*noun*)

Cornwall, Devon, Dorset, Gloucestershire, Hampshire, Herefordshire, Ireland, Isle of Wight, Kent, Somerset, Surrey, Sussex, Wiltshire

Shelter, protection from the wind. From the Isle of Wight: 'Let's get into the lewth'. It's originally an Old English word, which came to be used across the whole of southern England, and travelled across to Ireland. Adjectives were *lootheed* and *lewthy* for a place that was warm and snug. From Somerset: 'a proper loothy spot'. In a general sense it was used for anything that provided warmth, such as coats, stoves, and the sun. A thin coat would have 'no lewth in it', they used to say in Wiltshire.

licksome (*adjective*)

Cheshire, Derbyshire, Flintshire, Herefordshire, Lancashire

Pleasant, agreeable, amiable; handsome, neat. From Lancashire, on an array of stalls in a market: 'Such licksome stuff aw ne'er did see i' Englondshire afore'. A good-looking person would also be described as licksome, as would a handsome animal. In Cheshire it was chiefly used for places, such as a 'licksome garden'. The origin is apparent in the spelling *likesome*, which had some currency in the sixteenth and seventeenth centuries, and which was common in Yorkshire in the sense of 'desirable, loveable'.

lig (*verb or noun*)

Norfolk, Suffolk

To carry with difficulty; to pull, drag heavily. From Norfolk: 'They ligged the ground rope in'. You could also *liggle* it. As a noun, *lig* meant a heavy load, or the lift or pull you'd have to perform to move it. In Suffolk, something might be given 'a good tidy lig'. There's a phonetic link to *lug*, a borrowing from Old Norse in the Middle Ages, which came to be much more widely used throughout the British Isles.

like-shence *or* likshence (*noun*)

Bedfordshire, Northamptonshire

Likelihood, chance. From Northamptonshire: 'No likeshence of his coming to-day'. A blend of *likelihood* and *chance*, which seems to capture a meaning somewhere between probability and possibility. 'There's a likechance of rain'. Will it rain? Maybe, maybe not.

limbless *or* **limless** (*adjective*)

† Dorset, Isle of Wight, Somerset

Past repair, all to pieces, utterly destroyed. From the Isle of Wight: 'Git out o' the way or thee'st be knocked limless'. Standard English used the word too, but literally.

limpsy *or* **limsy** (*adjective*)

† Essex, Hampshire, Norfolk, Suffolk, Sussex

Limp, loose, flabby; idle, lazy. From Norfolk: 'A loose lazy fellow is said to be a limpsy rascal'. But a damaged arm might also be described as limpsy, as would a lazy way of walking or a plant that failed to stay erect. From Essex: 'D'yer see them feathers stickin' in her 'at? They're limsy'. The word has also been recorded in some American dialects.

linnard (*noun*)

† Somerset

The last to finish a meal. It appears that, when working in the field, the man who finished his meal last had to do all the clearing away of the remnants. 'Thee beest linnard'. The origin isn't known. I suspect a link with an Old English verb – perhaps *linian* 'leave' or *linnan* 'cease'. The -*ard* ending has the sense of 'one who does what is discreditable', as in *drunkard, laggard,* and *sluggard*.

lobstropolous (*adjective*)

Northumberland

Loud, mischievous. From a Tyneside song: 'Lobstrop'lus fellows we kicked them'. It's an adaptation of *obstreperous*, with the addition of *lob* 'lump', widely used in the North of England to describe someone who was clumsy or idle, especially if they were also well built.

logaram (*noun*)

Bedfordshire, Northamptonshire, Rutland

Balderdash, rubbish, nonsense; a long story somewhat embellished. From Rutland: 'They've been saying ever such logarams'. It's recorded in Bedfordshire in the spelling *lockrem*, but the other form shows its unusual etymology more clearly. It is from *logarithm*.

longcanny (*noun*)

Northumberland, Yorkshire

The limit of endurance; the end of one's financial resources. From Yorkshire: 'Thee keep thi brass in thi pocket, he's allus at the long canny'. A woman in the advanced stages of pregnancy was said to be 'on the longcanny'. And you could use the word to describe the feeling of exhaustion at the end of a very long journey or of reaching your limit when trying to lift a collection of especially heavy objects. Its origin lies in the phrase 'long as I can'.

looby (*adjective*)

Cornwall

Of the weather: warm, muggy, misty. The word is from Old Cornish *loob*, meaning 'slime, sludge', and commonly encountered in the tin-mining industry, where it referred to the vessel that receives the unwanted earth after the tin has been removed. *Lubricate* is related.

lorricker (*noun*)

Cumberland, Lancashire, Westmorland, Yorkshire

The tongue; the mouth. From Yorkshire: 'Oppen thi gob an' shooit aht thi lorriker.' The word has the same probable origin as in *lally-wow*: the mouth is the place where you 'lall' and your tongue the thing you lall with. In the north-west, you would hear it also as *lallacker*. The switch between *l* and *r* often takes place among dialects.

lozzuck *or* **lossack** (*verb or noun*)

Cheshire, Lancashire, Shropshire, Staffordshire

To lounge, loll, idle, loaf. From Staffordshire: 'Do' come lossackin' about here, I'm busy.' If you were 'doing a lozzuck' you were having an idle time. From Lancashire: 'Th' day after we did a lozzick, oitch [each] gooin his own road, an' spendin his time as he'd a mind.' Origin unclear, but possibly related to *loose* or *lose* – as in 'at a loose end'.

lumrified (*adjective*)

Wales

Of a room: in disorder. From Pembrokeshire. 'She be'n't a good hausekeeper at all; every room is lumrified'. The source is probably *lumber,* in its sense of 'useless odds and ends'. The *b* was often dropped in dialects. In Yorkshire, for example, *lumber* was sometimes written as *lummer.*

M

madancholy (*adjective*)

Lancashire, Yorkshire

Very vexed, sulky. From Yorkshire: 'Shoo'd be as madancholy as owght [anything] if tha wor to tell her shoo'd a wart ov her nooase [nose].' It's an ingenious adaptation of *melancholy*.

maggle (*verb*)

Gloucestershire, Oxfordshire, Worcestershire

To worry, tease; tire out, exhaust. From Oxfordshire: 'I be maggled to dyeath' – said especially if one is hot and tired. The origin isn't clear. There may be a link with *mangle*.

mang (*noun or verb*)

Devon, Durham, Leicestershire, Lincolnshire, Northamptonshire, Northumberland, Scotland, Somerset, Wiltshire, Yorkshire

A mixture, a confused mass. From Leicestershire: 'All of a mang, loike'. The word is from Old English *gemang*, 'mixture, union'. As a verb, it meant 'mix together, mess about'. From Somerset: 'The bags was a bust, and zo the zeeud [seed] was a-mangd all up together'. It was also what would be said if someone touched food with the hand – such as choosing a piece of cake and then changing your mind. From Northumberland: 'Tyek the piece o' cyek ye mang'd forst'. And the outcome after producing a confused mass of something? A *mangment*.

mattery (*adjective*)

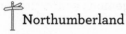 Northumberland

Wordy, loquacious. Said of someone making a fuss: 'What a mattery old man!' This is matter in the sense of 'content'. In Cumberland, if you got into a muddle while talking you would be *matter-fangled*.

mawbish (*adjective*)

Norfolk, Suffolk

Intoxicated. From Norfolk: 'Some o' they fellows 'll go home mawbish'. *Maw* was in general dialect use in Britain for a mouth or throat. It originally referred to the stomach of an animal, and when used for humans there was often a nuance of eating (or drinking) as much as possible, to stave off hunger (or thirst).

mettly (*adjective*)

Cheshire

Quick-tempered, irritable. 'He was very sharp an' snappy, was th' owd 'un [old one] – despert mettly'. It's a development of *mettle* (as in 'on your mettle'), which was used idiomatically across the North of England and Scotland in related senses. If you were *over sharp mettle* you were too hasty-tempered. If you were *mettle to your teeth* you were full of spirit.

middlemer (*adjective*)

Cumberland, Westmorland, Yorkshire

Central, middle; coming between the eldest and youngest in age. From Cumberland: 'Is that t'auldest lad er youngest?' 'It's nowder, it's middlemer'.

mim (*adjective*)

Berkshire, Cornwall, Durham, Ireland, Norfolk, Northumberland, Oxfordshire, Scotland, Suffolk, Yorkshire

Prim, demure; affectedly modest or shy; prudish. The word is imitative of the action of pursing up the mouth when behaving in this way. There's a Scottish proverb: 'Maidens should be mim till they're married, and then they may burn kirks'. And a sad tale from Berkshire: 'She zet there zo mim as I cood'nt get on no how, an' zo I got up an' come away'. The word gave rise to a wide range of expressions with similar meaning, such as *mim-mouthed*, *miminy-mouthed*, *mimmocky*, and *mimsey*.

mirligo (*noun*)
 Scotland

Dizziness, disordered vision. From Edinburgh: 'My own een [eyes] began to reel with the merligoes'. In the Shetland Isles the verbs *mirr* and *mirl* – both borrowings from Old Norse – were used to express notions of trembling and rapid movement. An alternative spelling shows a popular etymology: *merrilygo*.

miscomfrumple (*verb*)
 Northamptonshire

To rumple, crease. A local writer gave this definition: 'If one female sits so close to another as to rumple or crease her dress, by pressing or sitting upon it, she is said to miscomfrumple it.' The formation is echoed in other words from the same part of the country: see *discomfrontle*.

misword (*noun*)
 Berkshire, Cheshire, Dorset, Gloucestershire,
Herefordshire, Kent, Suffolk, Surrey, Sussex,
Warwickshire, Wiltshire, Worcestershire, Yorkshire

An angry, unkind, or abusive word; blame, censure, disagreement. From Warwickshire: 'He never gave me a misword all his life'. There are a dozen examples recorded, from Cheshire to Kent, all expressing the same sentiment – of never having had a row. Just one, from Dorset, suggests that relationships were not always so peaceable: 'But, look ee, I beaint a-gwine to take no miswords vrom thy vo'k [folk]'.

modge (*noun*)
Nottinghamshire, Warwickshire

Confusion; a state of dirt and disorder. From Nottingham-shire: 'The floor was all of a modge'. The word also turns up as a verb, describing the way someone gets into a muddle, especially in the phrase *codge and modge*. Advice to a Warwickshire seamstress: 'Don't codge and modge at that patch any longer'.

mome (*noun*)
Westmorland, Yorkshire

A fool, blockhead; a dull ignorant person. From the North Country: 'Away with this foolish mome!' It was also used as an adjective with the general meaning of 'dull'. Lewis Carroll thought it to be a nonsense word, when he talked about the 'mome raths' in his *Jabberwocky*. Humpty Dumpty isn't certain of its meaning: he thinks it might mean that the raths ('green pigs') had 'lost their way'. They wouldn't have found it nonsense up north.

mortacious (*adverb*)

Cheshire, Kent, Norfolk, Suffolk, Sussex

Extremely, exceedingly. From Sussex: 'He was so mortacious hungered he tumbled in de street'. It was a localized variant of *mortal* when used as an intensifier – as in Warwickshire: 'this is mortal poor beer' – which was widespread across the British Isles, and a feature of many American dialects.

motty (*noun*)

Cheshire, Derbyshire, Lancashire, Warwickshire, Yorkshire

A word, talk, speech, uttered opinion. From Lancashire: 'Thou'rt al'ays out wi' ty motty'. The word was usually heard in the expression *to put one's motty in*, 'to interfere impertinently in a conversation, stick one's oar in'. From Cheshire: 'What art puttin thy motty in for?' The origin is the French word *mot*, 'word, utterance', which arrived in English in the sixteenth century and soon came to be pronounced 'mott'.

muckment (*noun*)

Cumberland, Lancashire, Lincolnshire, Yorkshire

Dirt, mud, filth. From Yorkshire: 'Sam all weet [wet] an streaked wi' ashes an all sooarts o' muckment.' The *-ment* suffix is normally used to make an abstract noun from a verb (as in *astonish* > *astonishment*), but here, added to another noun, it adds a nuance of widespread presence. A floor covered in muckment is likely to be more messy – and more diversely messy – than one just covered in muck.

mulligrubs (*noun*)

 Berkshire, Cheshire, Devon, Essex, Hampshire, Lincolnshire, Norfolk, Nottinghamshire, Oxfordshire, Scotland, Shropshire, Somerset, Suffolk, Sussex, Warwickshire, Wiltshire, Yorkshire

A stomach-ache, the colic; any imaginary ailment. There was hardly a corner of the country that didn't use this word, which is recorded in an extraordinary variety of forms – *molligrubs, molligrumphs, moolygrubs, murdigrups*, and much more. From Berkshire: 'What's the matter with you – got the mulligrubs'. If you were *in the mulligrubs*, you would be low-spirited and sulky. It could also refer to an ill-natured person. From Devon: 'Her's a proper old mullygrub'. The word may come from a kind of grub that lives in the *mull* ('mould').

mumple (*verb*)

 Scotland

To seem as if going to vomit. *Mump* was widely used in England and Scotland to mean 'mumble', 'munch', and other effects involving the mouth, such as chewing, nibbling, and grimacing. If you suppressed a chuckle, you would be 'mumpling in the mouth'. And yes, *mumps* is related, the name coming from the swellings around the chin associated with the disease.

N

nang *or* **gnang** (*verb*)

† Cumberland, Dorset, Kent, Somerset, Sussex,
Westmorland, Yorkshire

Of a pain: to keep up a dull, continuous aching. From
Yorkshire: 'This old tooith is gnangin' at it agean'. It could
also mean 'complain, worry', like the crying of a fretful
child or the continual grumbling of an ill-tempered adult.
From Kent: 'He keeps on nanging at me'. The origin is
obscure: it may simply be a variant of *nag*, with the sound
of the *ng* adding an element of persistence.

nazzard (*noun*)

† Cumberland, Lancashire, Westmorland, Yorkshire

A silly, insignificant, mean person. As with other nouns
beginning with *n-* or *a-* (see *amplush, attercop*) people
often couldn't decide where to draw the line between the
indefinite article and the noun: is it *a nazzard* or *an
azzard*? The original form seems to be *nazzard*, as in this
Westmorland example: 'Didta ivver see sic a wurm itten

nazzard i' thi life?' The origin is obscure. There may be a link with French *nez*, 'nose' – perhaps recalling a contemptuous gesture made by flicking or waggling the fingers against the nose (as is still done today).

nesh (*adjective*)

Cheshire, Cornwall, Cumberland, Derbyshire, Devon, Dorset, Gloucestershire, Hampshire, Herefordshire, Lancashire, Leicestershire, Lincolnshire, Northamptonshire, Northumberland, Nottinghamshire, Scotland, Shropshire, Somerset, Staffordshire, Wales, Warwickshire, Westmorland, Wiltshire, Worcestershire, Yorkshire

Soft to the touch; delicate in health; brittle, crumbly; damp [weather]; dainty, timid. The Old English word for 'soft', *hnesce*, developed a wide range of senses throughout Britain, and entered American dialects too. From Somerset, about beans: 'They're too nesh to gather yet awhile'. From Herefordshire: 'The sheep be doing fairish, but some of the lambs be very nesh this time'. If you were *nesh-stomached*, you had a very delicate appetite. And if you had a timid-looking face, you were *nesh-phizzed*.

nickerers (*noun*)

Scotland

New shoes that make a creaking noise. The root of the word is *nick*, in its sense of 'make a clicking sound'. In

Scotland and the North of England, *nick-nack* was an alternative name for the tick-tock of a clock. In Cornwall, if you had *nickety-knock* you were having palpitations. The etymology isn't known. There could be a connection with horses: *nicker* was used throughout the British Isles to mean 'neigh', and the place in the mouth where the *gh* sound in *neigh* was made in Old English is the same as where a *k* sound was made.

niff *(noun)*

Cornwall, Devon, Gloucestershire, Shropshire, Somerset, Surrey, Sussex

A silent, sullen feeling of resentment; a quarrel. From Somerset: 'Let her alone, her've o'ny a-got a bit of a niff, her'll zoon come o' that again'. Someone offended would be *niffed* or *niffy*. The source isn't clear. It might have been a variant of *sniff*. In Sussex *niff* was used to describe a sniff or smell. It might also have been a variant of *miff*, 'huff'.

noggle *(verb)*

Cornwall, Hampshire, Shropshire, Wales, Yorkshire

To manage anything with difficulty; especially, to walk with difficulty because weak or heavily laden. From Pembrokeshire: 'I was main weak, I could hardly walk, but I noggled it somehow'. The speaker was thus feeling *noggly*. The word was also used for mental weakness – you could be *noggle-headed*, 'stupid' – and this may be the earlier usage, from *nog* or *knag*, a Germanic word meaning 'a block of wood', hence 'blockhead'.

noof (*adjective*)

Scotland

Sheltered from the weather, snug; neat, trim. From Galloway: 'The frien'ly firs, they keep it noof'. From Kirk-cudbrightshire: 'His wife was always bra' [smart] and unco' [very] noof'. A verb developed, 'to enjoy oneself leisurely'. From Lanarkshire, in an 1805 poem by George McIndoe: 'The laird sat noofan o'er his glass, / Baith [both] rum and brandy, Naething less, / Stood sparkling on the table'. The etymology is unknown. It could simply be a word that developed out of a noise – in this case, a sound expressing satisfaction.

norman (*noun*)

Oxfordshire, Shropshire, Suffolk, Yorkshire

A tyrannical person. From Suffolk, from a farm-labourer about a master credited with tyrannical conduct: 'Ah, he's a reg'lar Norman, he is'. This presumably dates way back to 1066. I place myself in some danger by including this entry, as it is my untyrannical wife's maiden name.

novels (*noun*)

Scotland

News, tidings. This sense of the noun was widespread in Britain 200 years before it came to be used in the modern sense of a long fictional prose narrative, and it survived in some parts of the country. From Renfrewshire, an eighteenth-century letter-writer: 'When you favour me with a line, I'll be glad to have your thoughts of it, with all your novels'.

nunty (*adjective*)

Cumberland, Kent, Leicestershire, Lincolnshire, Norfolk, Northamptonshire, Northumberland, Nottinghamshire, Shropshire, Suffolk, Sussex, Warwickshire, Yorkshire

Of dress: stiff, formal, old-fashioned, precise. The word was most often used to describe the way a woman was dressed, but it could also be used for men, or a piece of clothing. From Leicestershire: 'A nunty little man', 'A nunty cap'. The word also developed some negative meanings, such as shabby or dowdy in dress, or cross and sulky in manner. From Sussex: 'Ye be middlin' nunty this marnin' seemingly; I doant known naun what's putt ye out'. The etymology is unknown. Another meaning of *nunty* was 'stout and short', which suggests it could have been a rhyming relation of *stunt* or *stump*.

nurble (*verb*)

 Westmorland

To wear away slowly. Of shoes: 'Thoo's nurbled thi shun off at t'teeas [toes]'. Like many such words, the origin is probably playfully imitative, following the pattern of *burble* (from *bubble*), with an association of *n-* with slowness (see *nang* above). We still invent words in this way: in cricket, a new colloquialism emerged in the 1980s, to *nurdle* – 'to accumulate runs slowly by working the ball away gently'. *The Times* reports that a batsman 'crept, nudged and nurdled his way towards the total'.

O

oamly *or* **owmly** *(adjective)*

Yorkshire

Unpleasant or hurtful to the feelings; lonely, dismal,
dreary. The word comes from Old Norse *omli*, 'poor,
wretched, miserable'. It would have been important not
to mix this up with the identical-sounding *homely*, pronounced with a dropped *h*.

obsteer *(adjective)*

Lincolnshire

Stubborn, sulky, awkward. 'Charlie's a real obsteer man,
bud he's noht so bad as his faather ewsed to be'. The word
is a blend of *austere* and *obstinate*. The *ob-* element was
widely used in dialects, as seen in Berkshire *obfusticated*
('confused'), Yorkshire *obstracklous* ('obstreperous'), and
a general use of *obstropolous* (again, for 'obstreperous') in
dialects in many parts of the English-speaking world.

oddlin *or* **oddling** *(noun)*

Cheshire, Leicestershire, Lincolnshire, Northamptonshire, Nottinghamshire, Shropshire, Warwickshire, Yorkshire

Any person or thing standing alone, seen as differing from others; the last remaining member(s) of a family or community. From Yorkshire: 'Apples is ommost deean [almost down], bud Ah think we've a few oddlins left'. From Leicestershire, of a solitary house remote from others: 'They live at an oddlins'. In Cheshire, an eccentric person was described as 'one o' God's oddlins'.

odocity *or* **docity** *(noun)*

Rutland

Ability, spirit, energy. 'I seems as if I hadn't the odocity to work or to eat or anything'. *Docity*, sometimes written as *dacity*, was much more widely used in dialects throughout the Midlands and the South of England, and travelled to America. The source is *audacity*, with the opening unstressed syllable dropped, as often happened in dialect usage (and in colloquial standard English too, as when *banana* is pronounced as *nana*).

onfeel *see* **unfeel**

onshooty (*adjective*)

Shropshire

Of vegetables: coming up irregularly in the rows. 'How are your turnips coming on?' a man is asked: 'Well, they bin mighty onshooty; they'n missed five or six butts [ridges between furrows] together'.

oob (*verb*)

Shetland Isles

To howl, moan, wail. Seals and dogs were especially heard to oob. Of a dog: 'He wid rin a bit afore me oobin' as he guid'. The word came in from Old Norse *op* (with a long vowel – 'ohp'), 'crying, shouting', but it had its parallels in Old English *wop* (also with a long vowel), 'clamour, lament'.

oobit *or* **woubit** (*noun*)

Derbyshire, Durham, Northumberland, Scotland

A ragged, unkempt, hairy person. From Northumberland: 'Get away, ye clarty [filthy] oubit!' It's an extension of the name of the long-haired caterpillar of the tiger-moth, also called a 'woolly bear' (*wolbede* in Middle English, which simplified in pronunciation to *oobit*). In Scotland, it was usually heard preceded by 'hairy'.

orp (*verb*)

 Scotland

To weep with a convulsive pant; more commonly, fret, chide. A common expression was to 'orp and pine'. And if you were *orpit*, you were querulous or fretful. From Aberdeenshire: 'Benjie was an orpiet, peeakin' [peevish] little sinner'.

otherguess (*adjective*)

Cumberland, Devon, Somerset, Wiltshire, Yorkshire

Of another kind or variety. It's an adaptation of *othergates* or *otherguise*, the older meanings of the second element being replaced by something more understandable. From Yorkshire: 'Them words hez quite an clear an othergaz meanin'. *Otherkins* was also used in Yorkshire with this meaning. In Devon, it was *other-lucker*.

owmly *see* **oamly**

oxter (*noun*)

Cumberland, Derbyshire, Durham, Ireland, Isle of Man, Lancashire, Northumberland, Scotland, Suffolk, Westmorland, Yorkshire

The armpit; the fold of the arm when bent against the body; the armhole of a piece of clothing. From Westmorland: 'Ah's as sair as can be under mi oxters whar mi jacket rubs'. Several compound words arose. If you were stiff in the arm and shoulders you were *oxter-bound*. To walk arm in arm with a person was to *oxter-cog*. *Oxterful* was an armful; *oxterdeep* was being up to your armpits; an *oxter-pouch* was a breast-pocket; an *oxter-staff* was a crutch. Idioms too: to bring someone a present was *to come with the crooked oxter*; if you were walking with a downcast head you had *your head under your oxter*. This widely used word comes from Old English *oxta*, 'armpit'.

P

paamus (*interjection*)

 Lancashire

A beggar's expression: 'palm us' – give us alms. In Furness, they remembered a beggar's rhyme:

Pity, pity, paamas,
Pray give us aamas;
Yan for Peter,
Two for Paul,
Three for God at meead us all.

pample (*verb*)

Norfolk, Suffolk

To trample lightly; toddle about – often said of animals or children. From Norfolk: 'They du goo pamplin' about i' the slush'. There was also an adjective: a *pampling* person was fidgety. The word seems to be a blend of *pamper* and *trample*.

parsed (*verb*)

Herefordshire, Norfolk, Westmorland,
Worcestershire

Nothing to do with grammar. This is to be married. It comes from an uncommon use of the noun *parson* as a verb. From Norfolk: 'Don't you wish you was passoned?' A wedding was *parsoning work*. From Westmorland: 'We went te t'chapel for t'parsonin' wark'.

partick (*noun*)

Lancashire, Yorkshire

A special friend, a crony. From Lancashire: 'He's an owd partick o' moine'. It's a shortened form of *particular*, and the full form was also used in the same sense, especially in the Midlands. From Northamptonshire: 'They are very old particulars'.

parwhobble (*noun or verb*)

Cornwall, Devon, Herefordshire, Shropshire

As a noun, a conference; as a verb, to talk continuously, so as to dominate the conversation. *Parle* and *parley* were widely used in England and Scotland for any kind of talk, gossip, or conversation. To *parleyvoo* (from French *parlez-vous*, 'do you speak') in some places, such as Cornwall, was to speak in any foreign language or simply to talk with fine big words. *Parwhobble* sounds like a playful variant.

peedle (*noun or verb*)

 Cumberland, Lancashire, Westmorland, Yorkshire

To look or creep slyly about. *Peedling* is 'peering', as a short-sighted person does. From Westmorland: 'Any hofe-wit can tell by thy peedlin' Thoo cannot crack [brag] mitch of thy seet [sight].' *Peedoddle*, 'dawdle', seems to be related. A Lincolnshire source talks of a man who 'stands peedoddling aboot, isted i' geetin on wi' ther work, and rammen [rushing] right strite inte it'. This is *pee* in the sense of *peer* – 'look closely and narrowly' or 'look with one eye' – perhaps from *pie* (the magpie), reflecting the way birds look around.

perjink (*adjective*)

Scotland

Exact, precise; particular; trim, neat. From Forfar: 'He was looking unusually perjink'. A person displaying these qualities would be 'a perjink'. *Perjinkities* were 'niceties, exact details'. But at the other end of the country, in Cornwall, *perjinkety* meant 'apt to take offence'. The *jink* element is probably imitative, with a sound expressive of smallness or nimble motion, as with *dink* and *jump*.

perqueer *or* **perqueerly** (*adverb*)

Scotland

Accurately, by heart. From Aberdeenshire: 'Ye maun gee your answer just perqueer'. The word could also be used as an adjective. From Banffshire: 'Him speak sae faire, him sae perqueer'. It's a French loanword, harking back to the period in the Middle Ages when the Scots and the French were especially close: *par coeur*, 'by heart'.

pettigues (*noun*)

Sussex

Troubles, worries. 'She's not one as would tell her pettigues to everyone'. The model would have been *fatigue*. The *pet* element is known as a separate noun (as in colloquial standard English, to be *in a pet*, 'a fit of peevishness, a childish sulk'). Dialects display a wider range of idioms, such as *at pet*, *in the pet*, and *take the pet*. From Yorkshire: 'He taks pet at ivvery thing yan [one] sez or diz [does]'.

picklick (*verb*)

Huntingdonshire

To pick over one's food in a fastidious, fault-finding manner. 'Now then, don't sit there mammocking [cutting into pieces] them air vittals over. If yer can't do arout [without] picklicking, you'll 'a'ter [have to] do arout grub altogether'. The word is a combination of *lick* and *pick* in its sense of 'choosy' (as in modern *picky*).

pious-high (*adverb*)

 Dorset

Sanctimoniously. 'Granty be a churchwarden, and do come to church so reg'lar, and holds up his nose pious-high'. *Pious* is from Latin, and originally meant simply 'devoutly religious', but in the seventeenth century it took on a negative meaning of 'hypocritically virtuous'.

pleep (*verb*)

 Scotland

To speak in a querulous, complaining tone of voice. The word was originally used to describe the chirping of a bird. From the Shetland Isles: 'a pleepin' an' a cheepin''. People would talk about the plaintive chirping of sea-fowl: 'da pleeps alang da shore'.

pload (*verb*)

 Cumberland, Northamptonshire, Northumberland, Scotland, Yorkshire

To wade through mire and water. From Northumberland: 'Fither'll hammer ye for ploading i' the broad witter'. It is an adaptation of *plod*, influenced by *load*. A *ploader* was a plodder, a hard worker.

plook *or* **plouk** (*noun*)

Cumberland, Northumberland, Scotland, Yorkshire

A pimple; a spot on the skin. A Scottish writer talks of someone 'whase face was fam'd through a' the shire for wrats [warts] and plouks'. The word is a borrowing from Scots Gaelic, and travelled south into England, generating a small family of related words. If you were covered with pimples, you were *plooky*, *plookit*, or in a state of *plookiness*.

pluffy (*adjective*)

Cornwall, Devon, Leicestershire, Scotland,
Warwickshire, Yorkshire

Fat, swollen, chubby; soft, porous, spongy. From Leicestershire: 'The monks at the Tin-meadows say they live on nothing but vegetables; how come they be so pluffy, then?' The word is from *pluff*, widely used in the British Isles in its sense of 'puff, blast, as of a slight explosion', but also influenced by *plump* and *puffy*. In its 'spongy' sense, it was usually applied to food, such as bread or vegetables.

polrumptious (*adjective*)

Cornwall, Kent, Lincolnshire

Restive, rude, obstreperous, uproarious. From Cornwall: 'I'll get the loan o' the Dearloves' blunderbust in case they gets polrumptious'. The word seems to be an inventive combination of *poll* ('head') and *rumpus*. The origin of *rumpus* is unclear; there may be a link to the dynamic action verbs *romp* and *ramp*.

ponommerins *(noun)*

 Cheshire

Light, fleecy clouds dappling the sky. 'I thought it wur goin' to rain, didna yo see those ponommerins this morning?' It's a pronunciation of 'pan-hammerings' – the cloud pattern was thought to look like the kinds of marking seen on a new pan.

poweration *(noun)*

Cheshire, Herefordshire, Shropshire, Staffordshire

A great quantity. From Cheshire: 'It cosses a poweration o' money'. From Shropshire: 'A poweration o' rain'. *Power* has a similar meaning in such expressions as 'a power of good' and 'live to a powerful age'.

preedy *(adverb)*

Cornwall

Easily, creditably. 'That lock goes mighty preedy'. 'She does it bra' [fine] and preedy'. The source is *pree*, a widely used verb which meant 'experience, attain', itself a shortening of *prieve*, which in turn was a variant of *prove*. A *preeing* was a testing. From Perthshire, a variant of a well-known proverb: 'The pruif o' the puddin's the preein' o't.'

prickmedainty (*adjective*)

Cumberland, Scotland

Finical in language and behaviour; conceited. From Ayrshire: 'Bailie Pirlet was naturally a gabby prick-me-dainty body'. *Prickmaleerie* was used in a similar way. The first element is *prick* in the related sense of 'adorn', as in Northumberland: 'She's a' preeked up wi' ribbons an' laces'.

prinkling (*adjective*)

Northumberland, Scotland

A pricking, tingling sensation. An obvious blend, the word suggests that people wanted something to express a feeling that combined the two sensations. It was used in a variety of circumstances. From Selkirkshire: 'a prinkling through a' my veins and skin like needles and preens [pins]'. From Ayrshire: 'a prinkling at the roots of his hair'. You could have a 'prinkling conscience', and, when in love, one cheek would 'prinkle' when touching another.

proggle (*verb*)

Durham, Leicestershire, Northamptonshire, Northumberland, Warwickshire, Westmorland

To goad, prick, poke about. The verbs *prod* and *poke* gave rise to many other variations, such as *prockle* and *proitle*. Further north, and into Scotland and Ireland, it was usually *proddle*. From Leicestershire, of someone searching for an eel: 'The' was progglin' about i' the mud fur't best paart o' haf a hour'.

pross (*noun*)

Durham, Lincolnshire, Yorkshire

A chat, gossip. The word was widely used, especially across the North Country. From Lincolnshire: 'Come and smoke a pipe, and we'll have a little pross'. To *hold pross* would be to have a familiar talk with someone. If you were a conversational type of person, you were *prossy*. The origin is an adaptation of *prose*.

puckeration (*noun*)

Lancashire

State of excitement, vexation. 'It's no use gettin into oather a tantrum or a puckerashun abeawt an accident o' this sort'. In Yorkshire it was *puckerment*; and *pucker*, in the same sense, travelled the world, including America and Australia. The source is *puck*, a name made famous through the fairy of Shakespeare's *A Midsummer Night's Dream*, but much more widely used in the sense of a mischievous or evil spirit. Its value as an expression of annoyance is well illustrated by its intensifying use, which of course has its echoes in other expressions today. From Derbyshire: 'Why the puck don't you let her out?'

purt *see* **apurt**

pussivanting (*noun*)
Cornwall, Devon

An ineffective bustle. From Cornwall: 'This 'ere pussivantin' may be relievin' to the mind, but I'm darned ef et can be good for shoe-leather'. The source is thought to go back to the fifteenth century, when King Edward IV sent messengers to stop certain sea-captains levying excessive taxes. The messengers, called *pursuivants* ('pursuers'), weren't very successful, hence the later dialect meaning, with its folk pronunciation. There were variants elsewhere, such as Wiltshire, where it turns up meaning 'a flurry' as *pussyvan* or *puzzivent*.

puzzomful (*adjective*)
Devon, Lancashire, Yorkshire

Poisonous, noxious; filthy, infectious; piercing, very cold; spiteful, mischievous – in short, a very negative word. The origin is a local pronunciation of *poison*. From Yorkshire: a dose of unpleasant medicine is called 'puzzumful stuff'; the weather has 'puzzomful winds'; someone is described as having 'a puzzumful tongue'.

Q

quabble (*noun*)

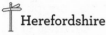 Herefordshire

Confusion. 'My head's all of a quabble'. To *quob* or *quop* was to tremble or throb. There are echoes of other imitative words, such as *wobble* and *quiver*. We find *quaggle* used in a similar sense further south.

qualmified (*adjective*)

 Norfolk

Sickly-looking. 'The mawthers [girls] all look so qualmified'. It's clearly from *qualm*, in its sense of 'sudden fit of nausea', a word that came to be adapted to any situation which might give rise to a feeling of faintness or sickness. In Northamptonshire, close or sultry weather was said to be *qualmy*.

quank (*adjective*)

🕇 Cheshire, Herefordshire, Shropshire, Warwickshire,
Wiltshire, Worcestershire

Still, quiet. From Shropshire: 'As quank as a mouze'. There was a verb use too, meaning 'subdue, quieten'. From Warwickshire, about a restive horse: 'You must quank him, or he'll master you'. Someone who settled disputes was a *quanker*. Further south, the word appears as *quamp*. From Gloucestershire: 'As quamp as a mouse'.

queechy (*adjective*)

🕇 Leicestershire, Somerset, Staffordshire,
Warwickshire

Sickly, ailing, feeble. From Somerset: 'They be a poor queechy old couple'. The origin isn't clear. I suspect it arose from people 'feeling queer', with the addition of an ending that often connotes unpleasant things, such as *blotchy*, *itchy*, *reechy*.

quezzen (*verb*)

🕇 Norfolk, Suffolk

To burn and smoke without flame. 'If the fuel be damp, the fire quezzens out'. You would also be quezzening if you smothered the fire with sand or earth, or tried to eliminate weeds by covering them in the same way. It's probably a local pronunciation and adaptation of *squeeze*, as *squezzen* is also recorded in Suffolk.

quiddle (*verb or noun*)

🚏 Cornwall, Dorset, Gloucestershire, Hampshire, Isle of Wight, Sussex, Wiltshire, Worcestershire

To make a fuss about trifles, fiddle about, fret. From Sussex: 'A quiddles over his cloase [clothes]'. As a noun, it meant a fussy, over-particular person, or a whim. From Wiltshire: 'She's quite a quiddle about the house'. From Cornwall: 'She's as full of quiddles as an egg is full of meat'. The word reached America. Ralph Waldo Emerson talks in his essay on manners from *English Traits* about the Englishman who is 'a quiddle about his toast and his chop'.

quignogs (*noun*)

🚏 Cornwall

Ridiculous notions or conceits. 'You're full of quignogs'. The origin isn't clear. It may well be an application of *whig*, an old name for a Nonconformist, with the *nog* element referring to the head (as with *noggin*, and compare *noggle*, above).

quizcuss (*noun*)

🚏 Cheshire

A meddlesome, inquisitive person. A tenant complained that his landlord was 'a regular quizcuss'. *Cuss*, of course, is from *curse*. In Lincolnshire, a prying person was called, simply, a *quiz*.

quob (*noun*)

Cornwall, Dorset, Gloucestershire, Herefordshire,
Isle of Wight, Leicestershire, Oxfordshire,
Shropshire, Wiltshire, Worcestershire

A marshy spot, bog, quagmire (also called a *quobmire*).
The word was widely used figuratively. If something was
in a mess or in a heap, it was said to be *all of a quob*. From
Cornwall: railway porters taking luggage out of a train
'pitch it down all of a quob'.

R

rackups (*noun*)

Cumberland, Isle of Man, Westmorland

The consequences of defeat or ill-doing. From Cumberland: 'Let every man stand his awn rackups'. The usage seems to have been proverbial. From the Isle of Man: 'But don't think I can't stand my rackups, as the saying is'. The origin lies in a game of marbles, called *rackups*. The loser places a marble between his fingers, just below the knuckles. The winner then fires another marble at it, usually hitting the knuckles. Ouch.

radgy (*adjective*)

Cumberland, Lincolnshire, Northumberland, Nottinghamshire, Yorkshire

Ill-tempered, angry, excited. From Lincolnshire: 'Them bairns was real radgy at the notion o' goin' to Cleethorpes'. The origin is *rage*. Also, in Yorkshire, if you were furious, you were *radged*.

rainified (*adjective or adverb*)

Herefordshire, Middlesex, Surrey

Inclined to rain. From Middlesex: 'I'm afeard it looks rather rainified this morning'. From Herefordshire: 'It blows rainified'.

rallack (*noun*)

Lancashire, Westmorland, Yorkshire

A roving character, an idle good-for-nothing. From Westmorland: 'He's nowt nobbut a gurt [great] rallak'. To be *on't rallak* was to be boisterously enjoying oneself. Also from Westmorland: 'Thi fadder's on t'rallak'. The word was widely used across the North Country. It's a variant of *rollick* (as in 'We had a rollicking good time'), which was probably a blend of *romp* and *frolic*.

ramfeezled (*adjective*)

Scotland

Exhausted with work. From Forfar: 'I'm fairly ramfeezl'd'. The result of your fatigue would be *ramfeezlement*. This is *ram* in its usual sense of 'act with vigour or energy'. *Feeze*, likewise, was a verb that had meanings to do with energetic action. The combination of the two suggests a really intense meaning for the word. If you were ramfeezled, you really were worn out.

randivoose (*noun*)

 Cornwall, Devon

A noise, uproar. From Cornwall: 'What's all the randivoose? I can't hear myself speak'. The origin is the French loan-word *rendezvous*. Such encounters, at least in the West Country, must often have been noisy affairs. Another attempt at the word in this part of the world was *rangevouge*. In Suffolk it was *renterfuge*.

rasmws (*noun*)

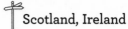 Wales

A mighty man – but usually with negative associations. From Cardiganshire: 'He is a rasmws of a man'. The Welsh spelling hides the origin, which is the name *Erasmus*. Whether the origin is the famous Dutch scholar or some unpopular local personality (Erasmus was quite a common first name in this part of Wales) is a mystery.

rickmatick (*noun*)

Scotland, Ireland

Concern, affair, collection. From Northern Ireland: 'I sent off the whole rickmatick'. From Forfar: 'Brocht the hale [whole] rickmatick clatterin' down on the floor'. People usually talked about 'the whole rickmatick'. This is *rick* in the sense of 'heap, pile' (as in *hayrick*), with the numerical sense of *arithmetic* not far away.

rifty (*adjective*)

Cheshire, Cumberland, Derbyshire, Durham, Ireland, Isle of Man, Lancashire, Leicestershire, Lincolnshire, Nottinghamshire, Scotland, Westmorland, Yorkshire

Causing a belch. From Yorkshire: 'This is rifty meat'. *Rift* in this sense is from Old Norse, where the related verb meant 'belch'. From Nottinghamshire: 'Parsnips allus make me rift'. *Rifty* could also be applied to anyone 'belching abuse'. And if you were *rifting-full*, you were totally replete.

rightle (*verb*)

Bedfordshire, Cumberland, Lancashire, Lincolnshire, Nottinghamshire, Rutland, Westmorland, Yorkshire

To set in order, put to rights. From Rutland: 'I'll take one o' thay old toobs [tubs] an' rightle it oop for the children's rabbits'. In Ireland, the corresponding verb was *rightify*: 'I wondher any one would throw away their time sthrivin to rightify you'.

ronkish (*adjective*)

Cheshire, Gloucestershire, Herefordshire, Nottinghamshire, Shropshire, Staffordshire, Warwickshire, Wiltshire, Worcestershire, Yorkshire

Mischievous, precociously wanton. From Warwickshire: 'He's a ronkish youth'. This is an adaptation of the adjective *rank* in its senses of 'cunning' and 'depraved', combining the two. From Nottinghamshire: 'Oh, the woman's a ronk un! Ivry child she's hed es bin by a different man'.

ronkle (*verb*)
Cheshire, Cornwall, Devon

To fester, be inflamed. From Cheshire: 'Aw geet a prick i' my thumb, an' it's done nowt bu' ronkle ever sin'. There was a figurative sense too: something can ronkle in one's mind. It's a local form of *rankle*.

roomthy (*adjective*)
Berkshire, Leicestershire, Northamptonshire, Oxfordshire, Warwickshire, Yorkshire

Roomy. From Warwickshire: 'These housen is very roomthy.' The noun is *roomth*, 'a room' – not to be thought of as a lisped version of *rooms*. In Pembrokeshire, they said *roomly*.

rox (*verb*)
Gloucestershire, Herefordshire, Isle of Wight, Leicestershire, Northamptonshire, Warwickshire, Worcestershire

To soften, decay. From Leicestershire, of a gatepost: 'It roxes at the end, loike'. Fruit would be said to rox, as would the ground after a frost, and a dry cough when it begins to loosen. The origin isn't clear, but there may be an association with *rot*.

rumgumption (*noun*)

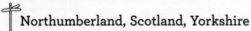 Northumberland, Scotland, Yorkshire

Rough common sense, shrewdness. From Aberdeenshire, a poetic couplet: 'Sure it wad be gryte presumption, / In ane [one] wha has sae sma' [such small] rumgumption'. *Rumgumptious* is the adjective, meaning 'shrewd, witty', but also sometimes 'pompous, forward'. *Rum* often had this double application, expressing both positive and negative meanings. For some people, to call a man a *rum cove* was to praise him; for others it was to criticize him. *Gumption*, 'common sense', seems to be Scots in origin. A further variant in the North Country was *rummelgumption*.

ryntle (*verb*)

Yorkshire

To roll about in a chair in a lazy manner – the *ry-* rhymes with *my*. 'She ryntled abaht like a cah [cow]'. The origin isn't known. It could be a variant of *round*. Or it could be related to *rindle*, which describes the gentle flowing of a small stream (*rynel* in Old English).

S

saidment (*noun*)

 Yorkshire

A report or statement about someone, especially if malicious. 'The's been monny saidments aboot him, and noo the'v cum'd thrue [now they've come true]'. Across the Pennines, in Lancashire, a report or statement previously made was a *said-so*.

sammodithee (*noun*)

Norfolk, Suffolk

A form of reply to a salutation or toast: 'the same unto thee'. A traveller in Norfolk reported that, when saying 'Good evening' to a ploughman or boatman, this was the expression he most often heard by way of response.

sang (*noun*)

Cumberland, Durham, Gloucestershire, Ireland, Lancashire, Lincolnshire, Northumberland, Scotland

An oath – literally, a translation of the French word for

'blood'. It was usually heard as part of a phrase, such as *my sang* or *by my sang*. From Dumfriesshire: 'My sang, ye weel deserve a thackin'. A variant in Northumberland was *sankers*.

scarcify (*verb*)
Lancashire

To absent oneself. 'Aw think aw'll scarcify misel' – make myself scarce. *Scarce* proved to be a useful source for several dialect words, such as Somerset *scarceheed* ('scarcity'), south-east England *scarcey* ('scarce'), and Irish *scarcen* ('lessen the number').

scaum (*noun*)
Yorkshire

An appearance of scorn; scornfully abusive language – the vowel-sound is the same as in *lawn*. 'I reads Mrs. Burneston like a book, for a' t'scaum in her face'. The word is a phonetic adaptation of *scorn*, which in dialects had a wide range of meanings. It could be used lightly, in the sense of 'banter'. And to *think scorn of* someone was to think lightly of them. *Scaum* was used in similar ways. 'That's like his scaum' – meaning the trick of his talk, being insincere in his speech.

scawvey *see* **scovy**

sclatch *or* sklatch *(noun)*

An unseemly mass of something semi-liquid; a large clot of mud or filth; a large spot or mark on the skin. From Banffshire: 'He hiz a red sklatch on's broo'. The word also developed an intensifying sense, meaning 'heavily, violently': 'He fell sklatch our o' [over on] the green'. And it would have been quite an insult to call someone 'a sclatch'. The word is probably echoic in origin, with influences from related words such as *squelch* and *patch*. Several similar-sounding words expressed the same meanings, such as *sclute* and *sclyte*.

sclum *or* sklum *(noun or verb)*

Cornwall, Devon

To scratch as a cat – or like a cat. From Devon, a child's nurse said, apologizing for her untidiness, ''Tis the baby sklummed me'. The result would have been a *sclum* on her face. A spiteful person was a *sclum-cat*. Probably it's an adaptation of *scratch* with an echoic ending suggestive of unpleasantness (as in *glum, slum, scum,* etc.).

scoll *or* skole *(noun or verb)*

Scotland

The drinking of health, a toast. It's interesting to see this well-known Scandinavian word (e.g. Danish *skaal*, 'cheers') establishing itself in Scotland, and I wonder if it ever had any usage south of the border in Danish-influenced areas.

It was also used as a verb: people would talk about 'scolling and drinking'.

scomfish *see* **scumfish**

scorrick *or* **skorrick** (*noun*)

 Cheshire, Cumberland, Derbyshire, Dorset, Gloucestershire, Hampshire, Lancashire, Lincolnshire, Norfolk, Northamptonshire, Nottinghamshire, Scotland, Somerset, Staffordshire, Suffolk, Warwickshire, Westmorland, Worcestershire, Yorkshire

A fragment, the least particle. From Yorkshire: 'Ah thowt ther would ha bin summat left, bud ther waant a scorrick'. The word turns up with several vowels, such as *scerrick*, *scirrick*, and *scurrick*, and the spellings with *k* are as common as those with *c*. In the form *skerrick*, it came to be common in colloquial Australian speech. The etymology isn't known, but it sounds like a word with an Old Norse origin.

scouk *or* **skook** (*noun or verb*)

 Scotland

To scowl, look angry; go about in a secret or guilty manner. Scots poet James Hogg curses Whigs (in 'Geordie Whelps' Testament') and the way 'They girn, they glour, they scouk, and gape'. As a noun, it was a frown or scowl. From Aberdeenshire: 'Wi' horrid scouk he frowns on a''. The word is a local pronunciation of *skulk*.

scovy *or* **scawvey** *or* **skovey** (*adjective*)

Cornwall, Devon, Somerset

Uneven in colour, blotched, streaky, mottled, smeary. The word was usually applied to cloth. From Somerset, of a piece of woollen stuff: 'I can't think how 'tis, he come out so scovy'. But anything that was badly cleaned or painted would attract the word. From Devon: 'You haven't half cleaned this window; it's all scawvey now'. The etymology isn't clear. It may be related to *scove*, used in Cornish tin mining for ore that is so pure that it needs little cleaning. The development of a meaning opposite to its original is common enough in the history of words (as today, when *wicked* started to mean 'excellent').

scranky *or* **skranky** (*adjective*)

Lincolnshire, Scotland, Yorkshire

Lean, lank, thin, scraggy; withered, wrinkled. From Scotland: 'He is a shrewd, canny-going, skranky-looking individual'. Badly formed writing would also be described as scranky. The word is probably related to *shrink*, as there was often an alternation in early English between words beginning with *sk-* and those with *sh-*. (We see it in place-names too, such as *Shipton* and *Skipton*.)

scrattle (*verb*)

Bedfordshire, Cheshire, Cumberland, Derbyshire, Lancashire, Leicestershire, Shropshire, Warwickshire, Yorkshire

To labour hard; to scrape and save. From Leicestershire: 'The' manage to scrattle on' – gain a precarious livelihood. The origin is *scratch*, which became *scrat*, and then (adding a nuance of repeated action) *scrattle*. It was first used to describe the repeated scratching of an animal, such as a hen in a yard or a dog at a door; but it also developed a range of figurative senses. Writing with a pen was sometimes described as *scrattling*, from the scratching sound it made.

scrawlation (*noun*)
Devon

Confusion, disorder. 'Aw, yer's a purty scrawlation. 'Tweel take me an hour to put thease drawer strite and vitty [fit]'. One of the meanings of *scrawl* was 'toss about in a disorderly way'. Corn blown about by the wind was said to be *scrawly*.

scrigs (*noun*)
Wiltshire

Small fruit left after the gathering of a crop. Anyone who sees an apple tree at the end of a growing season will find the word useful. It has a phonetic origin, with the short *i* vowel expressing a feeling of smallness, seen again in *scriggins* (the same sense) and *scriggle* (an undersized apple left on a tree as worthless), recorded also in Gloucestershire and Worcestershire.

scrink *or* **skrink** (*verb*)

Cornwall

To wrinkle, screw up, especially to peer with half-closed eyes. 'Yiew may winky and skrinky as long as yiew do plase'. A related verb was *scrinkle*, also recorded in Norfolk and Suffolk, where the sense was more 'shrivel up', as might be said of old fruit. The forms are clearly of phonetic origin, and related to such verbs as *screw* and *wink*.

scroggins (*interjection*)

Westmorland

An exclamation of astonishment. The word may simply be an invented form, but it could also be a distant echo of *God*, via *Gog* and other phonetic modifications to form a euphemism – in much the same way as we have *gosh*, *golly*, and others. There may even be a link with one of the phrasal euphemisms, such as *gadzooks* ('God's hooks', i.e. nails). In nearby Cumberland, another oath was *scurse* ('God's curse').

scrunty *or* **skrunty** (*adjective*)

Cumberland, Ireland, Lancashire, Northamptonshire, Northumberland, Scotland, Yorkshire

Stunted in growth, thin, meagre, scraggy, worn down. From Northumberland: 'He's a poor, sitten-on, scrunty body'. Trees and plants could be scrunty, as well as people. The 'meagre' nuance led to a sense of meanness.

From Cumberland, said to a niggardly tradesman: 'Divent be saw scrunty'. The base of the word, *scrunt*, seems to be an adaptation of *scrunch* or *stunt*, or probably both.

scumfish *or* scomfish (*verb*)

† Cumberland, Durham, Lincolnshire, Northumberland, Scotland, Westmorland, Yorkshire

To suffocate, stifle, choke – generally used of heat, smoke, or a bad smell. From Lothian: 'Fair scomfist wi' the heat'. From Yorkshire: 'T'grund's scumfish'd wi' wet'. The word looks as if it is made up of *scum* + *fish*, hence the bad smell, but the etymology is more pedestrian. The alternative spelling provides a clue. *Scomfish* was a shortened form of *discomfish*, which in turn was an adaptation of *discomfit* ('defeat'), a relative of *discomfort*.

seemth (*noun*)

† Northamptonshire

Appearance. Another instance of the largely disappeared *-th* noun ending in English (see *chilth*, *dryth*, *feelth* above). 'By the seemth of the thing'.

semi-demi (*noun*)

† Lincolnshire

One who is weak, small, or of no account. 'I call him nobbut a semi-demi wheare a real man cums'. The source is musical: *semi-demi quaver*.

shakaz (*verb*)

Cheshire

To shirk work. 'Raggazin' [wandering around] and shack-azin' about'. The adjective *shackazing* also developed the sense of being untrustworthy. The word may be no more than a local variant of *shirk*, but *shackle* also has some relevant senses to do with idling about. *Shackle-bag* was recorded in Cheshire and in Somerset, meaning 'a lazy loiterer'.

shalligonaked (*adjective*)

Cheshire, Cornwall, Dorset, Shropshire

Of clothing: flimsy, light, scanty; unsuitable for outdoor wear. From Shropshire: 'Whad good ool that fine shalligo-nakit thing be? – it'll cut a poor figger on a wet day'. It's unusual to see a whole sentence turn into an adjective, but the variant spellings around the country, such as *shally-go-naked*, suggest it was quite a popular expression.

shazzaas (*verb*)

Devon

To make a curtsey, to be extremely polite. 'You should have zeed Mary Andrews come into the room a-shazzaasing avore her betters like the first lady in the land'. The un-usual spelling hides the source: *chassez*, from the French verb *chasser*, 'to chase'.

sheddle (*verb*)

Yorkshire

To swindle. From Yorkshire: 'Thar't a bonny un' ar'n't tuh, to goa sheddle a chap art o' fifty pound'. The swindler, or a defaulting debtor, was a *sheddler*. To *sheddle out* was to back out of an engagement in a dishonourable way. To *sheddle off* was to take a hurried departure. All derive from a dialect version of *schedule*.

shivvy (*adjective*)

Yorkshire

Feeling rough, as caused by a new undergarment. 'This calico is rather shivvy'. The source is a Germanic word, *shiv* or *shive*, describing the husk of oats, or a particle of chaff, and thus any small piece of a foreign substance that gets into woollen materials.

shobble (*verb*)

Worcestershire

To do odd jobs. 'E've got a 'oss an' cart, an' does bits o' jobs for one an' the t'other, an' gooes about shobblin' like'. He's a *shobbler*, in other words – someone with no regular employment. The etymology isn't clear. It may be a pronunciation coming from *job*.

shram (*verb*)

Berkshire, Dorset, Gloucestershire, Hampshire, Isle of Wight, Norfolk, Somerset, Sussex, Warwickshire, Wiltshire

To shrink with cold, benumb, stiffen. From the Isle of Wight: 'Let's get avore the fire, vor I be ver' neer shrammed'. To be *all of a shram* was to be benumbed with cold. The source seems to be an Old English verb, *scrimman*, with the same meaning, which had a past tense *scramm*. The pronunciation shift between *scr-* and *shr-* is found in several words from that period.

shucky (*adjective*)

Berkshire, Gloucestershire, Hampshire, Herefordshire, Kent, Lincolnshire, Norfolk, Nottinghamshire, Suffolk, Surrey, Sussex, Wiltshire, Worcestershire

Rough, uneven, jolting. From Berkshire: 'The roads be's so rucky and shucky'. The source is a dialect pronunciation of *shake*. We see the same sort of transfer of meaning in the use of *shucky* to talk about the weather: unsettled, windy, cold – anything that might cause you to shiver. From the Midlands: 'It's impossible to do any hay-making this shucky weather'. In the south-east they preferred *shuckish*.

shupernacular (*adjective*)

Shropshire

Superior, excellent. Apparently the word was used to describe any liquor of a fine quality. It's presumably an invention combining *super* and *spectacular*. The *sh*-onset possibly has an alcoholic rather than a philological origin.

sidth (*noun*)

Lancashire, Norfolk, Shropshire, Yorkshire

The length or depth of a side of something. A Shropshire source shows three of the rare *-th* nouns in English brought together: 'Lenth, width, and sidth'. The pronunciation is like *Sid*, following the pattern of *wide > width*. In Norfolk, the word was shortened, presumably for ease of pronunciation: 'The width and the sith'.

sillified (*adjective*)

Oxfordshire, Surrey

Silly, foolish, delirious. From Surrey: 'He was quite sillified yesterday'. *Silly* turns up in many combinations. In Cumberland, a simpleton was a *sillican*. In Norfolk and Suffolk, an impertinent or impudent person was a *silly-bold*.

skenchback (*adjective*)

Northamptonshire, Yorkshire

Having strong personal or family characteristics; remarkable in appearance, easily recognizable. From Yorkshire: 'I should know yon man anywhere; he's skenchback enough to pick out of a thousand'. The word seems to be related to *askance*, and also to *sken*, a form of *squint*, which both suggest something that is visually out of the ordinary.

skitterways *or* skitaway (*adverb*)

Isle of Wight, Surrey, Sussex

Diagonally, from corner to corner, irregular, not straight and even. From Surrey: 'There, look at old Johnny! He will go skitaway over that there grass-plot'. *Skitter* was a local pronunciation of *scatter*, a verb that was used in a broad range of senses, all to do with unpredictable movement. Talking of which, *skitterful*, *skitterish*, and *skittery* were widely used in England and Scotland for a bout of diarrhoea, though here the origin is more likely to be *squirt*. People still talk about having 'the skits' or 'squits'.

sklatch, sklum, skoll, skook, skorrick, skovey, skranky, skrink, skrunty *see* **sclatch, sclum, scoll, scouk, scorrick, scovy, scranky, scrink, scrunty**

skurreboloo (*noun*)

Westmorland

A chase, stampede. 'He gev it a regular skurreboloo fer aboot hofe an hoor'. The word is an interesting combination of two forms, each of which has a rhyming repetition (or 'reduplication') in its history. *Scurry* seems to be a playful formation based on *hurry*, as in *hurry-scurry*. *Hullabaloo* shows the reduplication of a hunting call – *halloo-baloo*.

skype (*noun*)

Scotland

A mean, worthless fellow; a lean person of disagreeable manner and temper. From Selkirkshire: 'If he durst I would claw the puppy hide of him! He is as great a skype as I know of'. The dialect meaning was presumably unknown to the founders of a well-known internet messaging service.

slamp (*adjective*)

Derbyshire, Lancashire, Yorkshire

Soft, loose, empty, tottering. From Derbyshire: 'As slamp and wobbly as an owd corn boggart [scarecrow]'. If you were clumsy you were *slampy*. Shoes were said to *slamp*, if you kept slipping on them. The word suggests a playful combination of *slack* and *limp*, but it could also be derived from *slump*.

slawterpooch (*noun*)

✝ Cornwall

A slovenly, ungainly person. 'Now, a slawterpooch Lisbeth certainly was not, a neater trimmer woman could hardly have been found'. A clue to the word lies in nearby Devon and Somerset, where *slatterpouch* was a dirty worn-out bag full of holes. *Slatter* was used all over the country in a range of negative senses, and gave rise to such words as *slattery* ('dirty') and *slattern*.

slench (*verb*)

✝ Cumberland, Durham, Lancashire, Westmorland, Worcestershire, Yorkshire

To hunt about privately with a view to stealing food, as a cat or dog – and thus, to pry about. From Westmorland: 'Wer olas hankerin [always loitering] an slenchan aboot'. A related word, *slenk*, suggests the origin: an Old English verb *slincan*, 'slink'. From Lakeland: 'He's slengkt hissel off ta bed without weshen [washing]'.

slod (*verb*)

✝ Norfolk, Suffolk

To wade through mire, melting snow, etc.; also, as a noun, the accretion of mud on one's boots. The word is probably echoic of the sound made by heavy feet. Further north, people would talk about *slodder* and *slodge* in the same way, and of course *sludge* and *slush* are known in standard English. In Lincolnshire and Norfolk, fen-dwellers, whose lives must have involved a lot of wading, were called *slodgers*.

slonky (*adjective*)

Ireland, Kent, Northumberland, Scotland

Having muddy places, wet hollows. From Northern Ireland: 'That slonky road'. *Slonk* was widely used to name any sort of depression in the ground. There may be a link with the Old English word *sloh*, 'slough', but – as with *slod*, above – there's probably an echoic element in the word, reflecting the sound of walking through mire.

sloonge (*noun*)

Yorkshire

A heavy blow with the open palm. 'Thoo'll get a sloonge ower heead thareckly [directly]'. The origin is probably *lunge* (originally a term used in fencing for a thrust), with influence from such words as *slap*. In the same part of the country we also find *slounging*, for any sort of heavy blow.

sloum (*noun*)

Cambridgeshire, Cumberland, Durham, Ireland, Lancashire, Lincolnshire, Northumberland, Nottinghamshire, Scotland, Westmorland, Yorkshire

A light doze – from Old English *sluma*, slumber, and found in a huge range of spellings, such as *slaum*, *slowm*, and *slum*. From Tim Bobbin, the Lancashire dialect-writer: 'Aw cudno [couldn't] tell whether awr in a sleawm or waken'. In Cumberland, the word was also used to describe the slow and silent motion of water in a deep pool. And there was a widespread use of *sloomy* to mean not just sleepy, but idle or dull.

smeddum (*noun*)

Bedfordshire, Durham, Scotland, West Country

Force of character, spirit, liveliness, intelligence. From Selkirkshire: 'I wish I could get Geordie weel droukit [drenched], it wad tak the smeddum frae him'. *Smeddum* was the name given to the powder or finest part of ground malt. It's from Old English *smedma*, 'fine flour'. In Yorkshire, it turns up as *smithum*.

smittling (*adjective*)

Lancashire, Lincolnshire, Yorkshire

Contagious, infectious. From Lincolnshire: 'It must be something smittling, for it has gone thruff [throughout] the house'. You would also hear it described as *smittlish*. The word comes from *smittle*, which adds a nuance of repeated effect to *smite* – as when we're 'smitten' with the plague, love, an idea . . .

snaff (*verb*)

⫟ Herefordshire, Leicestershire, Scotland

To sniff in a noisy, surly, or derisive manner. From Leicestershire, someone was described as 'snaffing and gurning [grimacing]'. An interesting development was a more positive sense, in the idiom *to say snaff if another says sniff*. It expressed the notion of 'consenting readily', and was especially useful when courting. From Herefordshire: 'If 'e said sniff, er'd say snaff in a minute'.

snaggilty (*adjective*)

⫟ Ireland

Likely to tear or cut. You might 'reive [tear] your ould coat-sleeve agin one of their bits of snaggilty wire'. The source is *snag*, an Old Norse word in its sense of 'sharp point, spike', which led to *snaggle*, and thence several derived forms, such as *snaggly* and *snaggish*.

snickup (*noun*)

⫟ Norfolk, Suffolk, Yorkshire

An indefinable illness, not easily cured. From East Anglia: to say of a man that he has 'got the snickups' means that he rather fancies himself ill rather than really being so. The word comes from the rhyming part of the expression *hiccup-snickup*. In Suffolk, a recommended cure for the hiccups was to repeat the following charm three times while holding your breath: 'Hiccup – sniccup – look up – right up – Three drops in a cup – is good for the hiccup'.

snoove (*verb*)
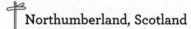
Northumberland, Scotland

To move with a smooth, equal motion. The word applied both to physical movement, such as walking with a steady pace, and more abstract states of affairs. From Dumfriesshire: 'Here in your dear hame Life snooves awa sae cannily'. If you really wanted to emphasize the steadiness, you could reduplicate. From Edinburgh: 'Up cam the two lights snoov-snooving, nearer and nearer'.

snot-snorl (*noun*)
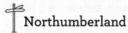
Northumberland

A kink or twisted bend in a rope or line – or, these days, a hosepipe. 'The rope's a' run inti snot-snorls'. *Snorl* and *snirl* were verbs meaning 'tangle', related to *snarl*, in its sense of 'make a tangle of' – in other words, 'snarl up'. *Snot* is probably a form of *snotch*, 'notch, knot'.

snozy (*adjective*)

Leicestershire

Comfortable. A woman, asked how her husband was, replied: 'Well, now, thankye, ma'am, he's very snozy to-day'. The etymology is unknown. It may be a blend of such words as *snooze* and *cosy*. Similar words with this meaning occurred elsewhere. In Dumfriesshire, a fat, comfortable man was called a *snoshie*.

snyirk (*verb*)
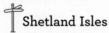 Shetland Isles

To creak, make a harsh grating noise. 'We heard dir aers [oars] snyirkin ipo' da kabes [rowlocks]'. It is virtually impossible to coin a word that exactly echoes the sound of oars moving against the sides of a boat, but this comes close.

soce (*noun*)
Cornwall, Devon, Dorset, Hampshire, Somerset, Wiltshire

A word used when addressing someone, either individually or as a group: Friends! Companions! Pronounced 'sohce'. From Wiltshire: 'Well, soce, an' how be ye all to-day?' From Somerset: 'Come, soce! here's your jolly good health!' The spelling varies a lot – for example, *soas*, *sose*, *zose*, *zuez* – but the sense is constant. The origin seems to be Latin *socius*, a word used when itinerant monks would address a congregation – the vocative form of the noun being *socii*. It's a usage that continued in standard English of a fairly academic kind in the sense of 'colleagues, associates'.

solacious (*adjective*)

 Scotland

Cheerful, comforting – giving solace. From Aberdeen-shire: 'So reall a freind, and so solatious a commrade'. It used to have quite a wide literary use, especially in the sixteenth and seventeenth centuries, but it gradually became dialectal.

solemncholy (*adjective*)

Scotland

Solemn, sober. 'He's a very solemncholy youth'. An obvi-ous blend of *solemn* and *melancholy*, but *solemn* in the sense of 'serious' or 'grave' rather than 'formal' or 'dignified'.

someness (*noun*)

Surrey

A sort, kind. 'Oi, minester didna mean it, oi'm a someness o' serten, or else he be goan wrung in's headworks'. It's unusual to find the *-ness* ending added to a grammatical word, but there are other cases, such as *much of a much-ness*.

soodle (*verb*)

Bedfordshire, Huntingdonshire, Lincolnshire, Northamptonshire, Rutland, Warwickshire, Yorkshire, and further north

To go unwillingly, linger, dawdle, saunter. From Lincoln-shire: 'Soodling along the hedge-side as if he hed nowt to do'. You would have a *soodly* gait. The etymology isn't known. It sounds like an echoic formation, perhaps influenced by *sidle*.

sot-whol (*noun*)
Cumberland, Westmorland

A place which was formerly a public-house, and now used for some other purpose. It is, quite literally, 'a hole for sots' – drunkards.

spaw (*verb or noun*)
Lancashire, Yorkshire

To go on a pleasure-trip, or go to the seaside. From York-shire: 'Yo're allus [always] spawin' off somewheare'. You would go to a *spawing-spot*. The source is *spa*, from the time when a trip to the nearest place with *spaw-water* was a regular day out for many.

splatherdab (*noun*)
Leicestershire, Northamptonshire, Warwickshire

A chatterer, gossip, scandal-monger. The act of dispensing news in this way is *splatherdabbing*. The first element is a variant of *splatter* – to splash water around, continuously and noisily. *Dab* also has a sense of 'spread about'. A related word in the same part of the country was *splatherdash*, describing a great deal of talk over a trivial matter. From Warwickshire: 'What a splatherdash you are making about it'.

splawt *or* splort (*verb*)
🪧 Derbyshire, Shropshire

To spread or stretch out the feet. From Derbyshire: 'He splorted all over the place'. The word is a variant of *splay*, which in turn is a shortened form of *display*. It was also used for people who talked at length, as in this Derbyshire example: 'Some o' these chaps is splortin' about as there should be a list o' poor folk'.

splute (*noun*)
🪧 Scotland

Someone who exaggerates. From Ayrshire: 'Robin was aye a terr'ble splute'. It's one of several dialect words that evolved out of *splutter*, referring to different ways of talking. In Berkshire, *splut* was recorded in the sense of 'make a fuss'. In Staffordshire it meant 'talk indistinctly'. *Spluther* was widely used in both of these meanings.

spong (*verb*)
🪧 Kent, Surrey, Sussex

To sew, mend, cobble, especially in a careless, clumsy manner. From Kent: 'Come here and let me spong that split in your gaberdin [smock]'. The etymology isn't known.

It could be related to the *spon* of *spon-new*, 'brand new', a southern variant of *span-new*, which came into English from Old Norse in the Middle Ages.

sprunt (*adjective*)

Northumberland, Oxfordshire

Smart, spruce; brisk, lively. From Northumberland: 'Mheyk thee sell [thyself] leuk varra sprunt'. The 'lively' meaning indicates the etymology. The word is related to *sprint*.

squinch (*noun*)

Devon

A narrow crack in a wall or a space between floorboards. 'I lost sixpence thro' a squinch in the floor'. A long narrow window could also be called a squinch, which helps with the etymology, as a similar aperture in a church, through which worshippers in the aisles could see the main altar, is called a *squint*.

squit (*noun*)

Hampshire, Norfolk, Suffolk, Warwickshire

Silly talk, nonsense. From Warwickshire: Your talk's all squit'. It was often used along with *slaver*, which also could mean (dribbling) nonsense. From East Anglia: 'Some people may look upon this correspondence as a lot of squit and slaver'. The etymology isn't clear, but there's a likely link with *squirt* and *skit*.

steehop (*verb*)

Devon, Somerset

To gad about, be frivolous, romp. From Somerset: 'Her is always steehopping about; better fit her would abide at home and mind her house'. The source is 'stay up', but popular usage has turned the second element into *hop*. The original sense is more evident when the word is used in the plural, meaning 'festivities'. From Devon: 'What with frawzies [feasts] and steops I had a jolly time'.

steg (*verb*)

Scotland, Yorkshire

To walk with long rapid strides, stalk about; be awkward in gait and manner, go about stupidly; stare vacantly. This plethora of meanings has a single source: they reflect the way a *steg* – a gander – moves about in a farmyard. It's an Old Norse word, meaning a male bird, which came to be used all over the British Isles. From Galloway: 'Auld Anton went stegging over the hills'.

sticklebutt (*adverb*)

Lancashire, Yorkshire

Headlong, with great impetuosity. From Yorkshire: 'He went stickle-butt into it'. The associated verb ('to run headlong at a thing') could also mean 'to persist in an opinion, whether right or wrong'. It's a combination of *stickle* ('stick') and *butt* ('head-thrust').

stime *or* styme (*noun*)

Cumberland, Durham, Ireland, Lancashire, Northumberland, Scotland, Westmorland, Yorkshire

The faintest form of any object, a glimpse; a gleam of light. It usually occurred in the phrase *to see a stime*. From Northern Ireland: 'It was so dark I couldn't see a stime before me'. But it could also be used for the notion of 'smallest particle'. From Northumberland: 'They hadn't a stime o' breed i' the hoose'. The etymology isn't known, but *stime* was also used for a disease of the eye, and along with *stimey*, 'dim-sighted', it suggests there may have been a link with *stye*.

stirriner (*noun*)

Yorkshire

A trial ball in a game, such as cricket. 'Send me a stirriner!' The notion seems to be one of 'stirring things up'.

stitherum (*noun*)

Lincolnshire

A long, dull tale. 'He tell'd me a straange stitherum all aboot a Rantin' preacher call'd Bywater'. *Stither* was common in this area to mean 'chatter' (possibly a variant of *stutter*). The ending is mock Latin. Whoever first thought this word up must have found his Latin lessons boring.

stog *or* stug (*verb*)

Berkshire, Cornwall, Devon, Dorset, Hampshire, Somerset, Wiltshire

To stick fast in mud. From Berkshire: 'Going athert [across] the field we was pretty near stogged'. It sounds like a neat combination of *stick* and *bog*. The alternative spelling, recorded in Devon, is also very close to *stuck*. There may also be a link with *stodge*, judging by the meaning of 'surfeit with food' recorded in Wiltshire: 'He could eat enough to stog a pig'.

stramash (*noun*)

Scotland, Yorkshire

A noise, uproar, tumult, hubbub; a disturbance, fuss. From Scotland: 'What a thing to mak' sic a stramash about!' It's a phonetic coinage, most likely using *smash* as its base and elongating the first syllable, and perhaps influenced by *slam*. It was also used to mean 'crashing about' or 'state of destruction'. From the North Country: 'He made a sad stramash amang the pots and pans'.

strollop (*verb*)

Lancashire, Wales, Yorkshire

To stride or walk about aggressively; to go about in an untidy, slovenly manner; to stretch the legs wide in sitting or standing. From Lancashire: 'And women strollopin' abeaut'. The noun shows a clear link with *trollop*, as well as *stroll*, used in dialects both negatively ('a slovenly, untidy woman') and positively ('a lively, extrovert girl').

struncheon (*noun*)

Lincolnshire, Yorkshire

A portion of a tune, a song; a portion of an address. From Yorkshire, of a nearby thrush: he was 'giving us a struncheon'. In a speech, if the speaker decided to introduce a parenthetical series of remarks, away from the main topic, that too would be called a struncheon, as would any long and involved story. The etymology isn't known. There may be a link with *truncheon*, which in its original sense meant 'fragment'.

strunt (*noun*)

Cumberland, Ireland, Northumberland, Scotland

A pique, a fit of ill humour or sulkiness. It was especially used in the phrase *to take the strunt* or *strunts*. From Selkirkshire: 'What gart [made] ye take the strunts o' the young laird?' – what upset you so much? The word was often linked alliteratively with another, as in these Scottish examples: 'Strunt and stirt are birds of ae feather', 'In a strunt or a strife he's regardless of life'. There could be a link with *stunt*, in the sense of 'arrested growth', used figuratively, with echoic influence from *grunt*.

stuffment (*noun*)
✝ Cumberland, Westmorland

Anything worthless; doubtful information. In Cumberland: 'A pedder [pedlar] wi' stuffment, she sauntert aw roun''. In Westmorland, an old man's tale was described as 'sad drowsy stuffment'.

stug, styme *see* stog, stime

suant (*adjective*)
✝ Cornwall, Devon, Dorset, Gloucestershire,
Hampshire, Isle of Wight, Somerset, Sussex, Wales,
Wiltshire

Smooth, even, regular – pronounced *syooant* or *sooant*. It could be used for land that was well ploughed, or a piece of cloth that was well woven, or a level road, or more generally, a well-modulated voice or gentle continuous rain. Anything that was pleasant or agreeable could be said to be *suant*. From Devon, a demure maid on her way to her wedding was described as 'a zuant blishin bride'.

From Cornwall, after drinking thirstily, you might hear someone say, 'Ah! that's suant'. The source is *suant*, a form of the Old French verb *sivre*, modern *suivre*, 'to follow', and thus 'be suitable'.

suddenty (*noun*)

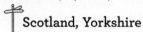 Scotland, Yorkshire

Suddenness, but only used in phrases, such as *upon a suddenty* or *all of a suddenty*. From Yorkshire: 'It cam doon amang us all on a suddenty'. From Scotland: 'My father's tongue was loosed of a suddenty'. The *-ty* ending seems to add a more concrete or dramatic nuance than is expressed by the abstract 'state of being' of *-ness*.

sumph (*noun*)

Scotland, Yorkshire

A stupid person, simpleton, fool, often used as an insult. From Aberdeenshire: 'Ye muckle useless sumph!' But it was used more darkly for any surly or sulky person, and one Scottish writer in an 1899 essay took pains to distinguish the two senses: 'A sumph is essentially an ill-conditioned fellow. Surliness is part of the character of a sumph. A simpleton can't help himself; a sumph is wilfully disagreeable'. The word is clearly phonetic in origin, the sounds themselves being used to convey the meaning.

surree (*noun*)

Ireland, Scotland

A social gathering. A Scottish writer describes it as an occasion 'where tea and speeches are given, a sort of homely conversazione, often in connexion with churches, Sunday schools, etc.'. An Irish writer sees it more as 'a subscription dance, a little more elaborate in its arrangements than are the kaleys [ceilidhs] or conversazioni'. The source is French: a *soirée*.

swaggle (*verb or noun*)

Cheshire, Cumberland, Gloucestershire, Norfolk, Shropshire, Suffolk, Warwickshire

To swing; sway to and fro, as a liquid in a vessel; to reel and stagger as a drunken man. From Warwickshire: 'What are you swaygling on that gate for?' The word is a blend, capturing a meaning intermediate between *sway* and *waggle*. In Shropshire it was also used for a child's swing.

swick (*noun*)

Scotland

A cheat, fraud, deceit. From Aberdeenshire: 'I expec'it a gowd [gold] watch, nae less. Sic [such] a swick!' A deceiver was a *swicker*, who would be *swickful* or *swicky*. The source is Old English *swician*, 'to deceive'. *Swick* also developed a positive sense: the art or knack of doing something properly. From Banffshire: 'He hiz a gey gueede [very good] swick o's wark'.

swid (*verb*)

Yorkshire

To tingle or smart, as a wound or burn. 'My hand swidded'. The source is an Old Norse verb, *sviða*, meaning 'to singe, smart' which is also recorded across the Midlands and North of England as *swidge*, *swidden*, or *swither*. The meaning is always one of superficial burning, admirably illustrated in this Yorkshire prayer: 'O, Lord, tak ahr Jack an' shak' 'im ower hell fire till his clogs drop off. But dunnot hurt him, Lord, nobbut gi'e im a bit ov a swither'.

swip (*noun*)
Scotland, Yorkshire

The exact image or likeness. From Yorkshire: 'The varry swip of his father'. The word was also used as a verb, 'to resemble closely'. Also from Yorkshire: 'They swip yan another varry mitch'. It's from an Old Norse word, *svipr* – 'likeness'.

swotchel (*verb*)
Isle of Wight, Oxfordshire

To walk lazily, roll in walking. From the Isle of Wight: 'Jack swotchels along the road as if a dedn't keer where a vell down or kept upright'. He would have been described as *swotchulting*. The etymology isn't known, but there are phonetic resemblances to several words of related meaning, such as *sway* and *lurch*.

T

taffety (*adjective*)

Devon, Dorset, Hampshire, Isle of Wight, Kent, Somerset, Surrey, Sussex, Wiltshire

Dainty, fastidious, particular, especially as regards food. From Dorset: 'He's so taffety, he won't eat what others will'. The word sometimes transferred to the eaten rather than the eater. From Hampshire: 'I could eat a taffety chicken' – tender, succulent. The word comes from *taffeta*, a fabric that evidently came to be associated with people of delicate taste and temperament.

tanklements (*noun*)

Lancashire, Yorkshire

Implements, accoutrements, litter, articles of finery. The notion applied to everything from tiny ornaments on a mantelpiece to large garden tools. From Lancashire: 'Let thi bits o' tanklements stop where they are'. The word is a variant of *tanglements*.

tantrups (*noun*)

Middlesex

Ill-humoured disturbances. 'Not that we means to make tantrups, you know'. This is a variant of *tantrums*, but with the additional nuance that the behaviour causes something to be 'up' – in a state of disorder. As for *tantrums* itself, the origin is unknown.

tawm (*verb*)

Cumberland, Lancashire, Scotland, Yorkshire

To fall gently asleep; swoon. From Yorkshire: 'Ah was just tawmin ower to sleep'. 'I'se like to tawme, this day's seay varry warme'. The word was also used as a noun to refer to a fit of drowsiness or faintness. The source isn't known, though there are several verbs in Germanic languages which could be related, such as Old Norse *talma*, 'hinder, obstruct' (*l* often changes into a vowel, as in *calm*, *palm*, etc.).

terrification (*noun*)

Scotland

Terror, or anything causing it. From Ayrshire: 'There was an outcry and a roaring that was a terrification to hear'. The -*ation* suffix forms a noun of action from a verb (as in *alter* > *alteration*), and thus adds an element of urgency that the basic noun, *terror*, lacks.

tharfish (*adjective*)

† Cumberland, Northumberland, Scotland, Yorkshire

Reluctant, unwilling, shy, of heavy countenance. From Yorkshire: 'She's rather a tharfish kind of a bairn [child]'. *Tharf* comes from an Old English word meaning 'un-leavened', where the bread had a heavy or stiff quality. People still talked of *tharf-bread* and *tharf-cakes* in the North Country. Physical heaviness later transferred to heaviness of spirit – a quality that could be attributed even to inanimate objects, as in this use of the associated adverb from Northumberland: 'She's gan varry tharfly' – said of a clock that appeared to be ready to stop at any moment.

thrawn (*adjective*)

† Durham, Ireland, Scotland

Perverse, obstinate, rebellious. From Northern Ireland, of a farmer: he was 'as thrawin' as a mule'. When used of the weather, such as 'a thrawn wind', it meant 'disagreeable, bitter'. A misshapen body, distorted face, or knitted brow would also be 'thrawn'. The common element is the notion of turning away from what is normal, and this was the earliest sense of the verb *throw*, from which the Scottish form *thraw* derives.

thrimble *see* **thrumble**

thring (*verb*)

Scotland, Yorkshire, and throughout the North Country

To press, push, squeeze; press forward, push one's way in. From Dumfriesshire: 'I shall just thring on here till I get desperate'. It comes from the Old English verb *þringan* (the initial letter was pronounced 'th') 'to press, crowd' – related to *throng*.

thruffable (*adjective*)

Yorkshire

Open throughout, and thus transparently honest and sincere. 'A thruffable sort of a body'. The source is *through*, with the *-gh* pronounced as *f* (as in *enough*): a thruffable person is someone who is capable of being 'seen through'.

thrumble *or* **thrimble** (*verb*)

Cheshire, Cumberland, Scotland, Yorkshire

To finger, handle, especially to work something between the finger and thumb to test its quality; fumble, grope. From Banffshire: 'He thrummilt i' the hole fir't a [for the] file afore he got it'. The word takes further the process seen in *thring* above. From the general notion of 'pressing', we get the more specific 'press between the fingers'.

thrung (*noun*)

Yorkshire

Trouble. 'I told mony a barefaced lee t' keep him out o' thrung at ooam [home]'. The word comes from Old English *þreagung* (the initial letter was pronounced 'th'), 'a threatening'.

thumbasing *see* **fummasing**

thusk (*noun*)

Lancashire

A blow, thump. 'Aw gan him a thusk i' th' yer-hole [earhole]'. To *leet thusk* was to 'come with a thump'. 'My heart leet thusk again mi soide at oych word loik a sledge hammer'. In Nottinghamshire and Lincolnshire, other forms were recorded that went in different semantic directions. If you were a *thusky* person you were big. Someone who did something with great energy was a *thusker*.

tiddytoit *or* **tiddytoity** (*verb*)

Yorkshire

To loiter, idle, waste time. 'Tom duz'nt loike mitch wark, he likes ta tiddytoity aboot'. A playful formation, it combines *tiddy* 'tiny' and *toit* 'totter'.

tiff-taffle (*adjective or verb*)

Nottinghamshire

To talk in a bantering manner, joke, make repartee.
'Wheniver A cums across 'im, A have a bit o' tiff-taffling
talk wee 'im'. *Tiff* normally had a negative meaning – a
slight quarrel or fit of temper – but here it has developed
a more positive tone, aided by the reduplication, which
usually adds an informal and playful tone to a word (as
with *chit-chat*, *bing-bang*, etc.).

timdoodle (*noun*)

Cornwall

A term of contempt applied to a stupid, silly fellow. 'Tha
gret timdoodle!' *Doodle* was a commonly used form in
relation to stupidity. Dr Johnson includes another,
fopdoodle, in his *Dictionary*. The *tim* part might be a
person's name, but – this being tin-mining Cornwall – it
could just as easily be a variant of *tin*, used by people who
looked down on the miners.

tiny-tiny (*interjection*)

Northumberland

A proclamation made when people find something
unexpected (such as a coin on the ground). The first one
to see it says 'tiny-tiny', and the first to claim it says
'miney-miney'.

toldrum (*noun*)

† Leicestershire, Nottinghamshire, Warwickshire, Yorkshire

Finery. From Yorkshire: 'Dressed up in her toldrums'. In Lincolnshire, if you were gaudily attired you were *toldered* or *tawdered*, and the alternative spelling reveals the etymology. It is *tawdry* (short for *tawdry lace*, a silk necktie commonly worn by women in the sixteenth and seventeenth centuries), which became a general word for any kind of cheap or showy decoration. *Tawdry*, in turn, is short for *St Audrey*, the patron saint of Ely, who, according to Anglo-Saxon historians, adorned herself with fine necklaces in her youth, and died of a throat tumour (which she considered a just punishment).

toober (*verb*)

† Northumberland, Scotland, Worcestershire

To beat, strike, shake. In a Scottish version of St Matthew's Gospel (24:49), the bad servant 'Sall begin to toober his fellow-servan's'. It's a development of *tabor*, a small drum, widely used across the Midlands in the sense of 'knock', and used as a noun as well. In Worcestershire: 'Thur comed a tabber at the doore'.

toot-moot (*noun*)

Scotland

A low, muttered conversation; the muttering which begins a dispute. From Aberdeenshire: 'I thocht I heard a toot-moot of tha kin' afore I left'. *Moot* is a variant of *mute*. *Toot* is being used in the general sense of 'make a noise (in the manner of a musical instrument)', in much the same way as one can *trumpet* something around. There's a lovely old Scottish expression, *an old toot in a new horn* – stale news.

torfle (*verb*)

Cumberland, Durham, Lancashire, Northumberland, Scotland, Westmorland, Yorkshire

To pine away, decline in health; tire out. From Yorkshire: 'I'm ommast [almost] toffild wi' me long wauak'. There's also an adjective: 'That hen leeaks [looks] varry torfly'. The etymology isn't known, but there could be a link with *topple*.

tossicated (*adjective*)

Berkshire, Cheshire, Cumberland, Derbyshire, Devon, Gloucestershire, Herefordshire, Isle of Man, Isle of Wight, Shropshire, Somerset, Warwickshire, Westmorland, Yorkshire

Tossed about, disturbed in mind; harassed, worried; puzzled, tormented. From Shropshire: 'Poor owd Molly looks bad, 'er's bin sadly tossicated lately ooth one thing or tother'. The word was also used throughout the country in its original sense, an adaptation of *intoxicated*. From Warwickshire: 'I were raly only tosticated once in my life, and that were from having some gin in my beer'.

towardly *(adjective or adverb)*

† Berkshire, Cheshire, Cumberland, Derbyshire, Gloucestershire, Herefordshire, Lancashire, Leicestershire, Northamptonshire, Shropshire, Wiltshire

Docile, quiet, easily managed; kindly, well contented. From Herefordshire: 'A uncommon towardly pony; some is so frangy and untowardly'. It could also be an encouraging sign to a hopeful suitor. From Berkshire: 'She looked at un [him] a bit towartly'. It's unusual to see a preposition, *toward(s)*, becoming a full content word in this way.

toze *(verb)*

† Cheshire, Cornwall, Devon, Lincolnshire, Shropshire, Somerset

Disentangle, pull asunder. From Somerset, a nurse said of a lady's hair that had become matted: 'let me toze it out, a little at a time'. It's a variant of *tease*, in its earliest sense in the woollen trade of 'separate fibres'. And, as with *tease*, it developed a wide range of meanings. In

Shropshire, 'pluck with the claws': a cat would 'toze the cushion all to pieces'. In Cheshire, 'tide over a difficulty': 'We con maybe toze on a bit with it' – pull through.

tragwallet (*verb*)

Cheshire, Ireland, Scotland

To wonder about in a slovenly manner, gad about. 'I wonder at um goin' tragwallitin about the country'. This is *wallet* in the sense of 'traveller's bag'. *Trag* is a variant of *traik*, widely used in Ireland, Scotland, and the North Country with the same meaning. Its etymology is unclear. It may be related to *trudge*.

trangleys (*noun*)

Dorset

Rubbishy trinkets, such as broken ironmongery or bits of joinery, used by children as toys. 'I am setting his room in order, so that when he comes back he may find all his poor jim-cracks and trangleys as he left 'em'. The word was evidently attractive as a basis for playfulness. In Cheshire, a similar meaning is found in *tranklibobus* and the plural form *tranklibobs*. Further north, in Cumberland, Westmorland, and Yorkshire, they were *trankliments*. Still further north, in Scotland, they were *trantlums*. Further south, in East Anglia and Devon, they were *trinkums*. The origin is probably *trinket*.

trickumtrully (*adverb*)

† Oxfordshire

Used in the phrase *to play trickumtrully* – to play false, act unfairly. 'Did you ever know me for to play trickumtrully!' The second element is probably a variant of *truly*.

trimple (*verb*)

† Gloucestershire, Herefordshire, Shropshire, Worcestershire

To tread gingerly, as one with tender feet, or wearing tight boots. From Shropshire: ' 'Ow that chap trimples alung – 'e met be walkin' on sparables [shoe-nails]'. A further meaning, 'walk lamely', indicates the etymology: a combination of *tread* and *limp*.

tud (*noun*)

† Shetland Isles

A sudden squall; a sudden gust or blast of wind, snow, rain. 'Du ye no hear da wind. Yon's snawy [snowy] tuds apo' da lum [against the chimney]'. The word is a variant of *thud*. It could also be used to mean 'talk a great deal'.

tush (*verb*)

Gloucestershire, Herefordshire, Shropshire, Worcestershire, Yorkshire

To draw a heavy weight along the ground, drag anything too heavy to be carried. From Shropshire: 'If I canna carry 'em, be 'appen I can tush 'em alung'. The word is the action that is the opposite of *push*, from which it probably derives, influenced by *tug*. (*Tush* meaning 'buttocks' isn't related: that has a Yiddish origin.)

tut (*noun*)

Bedfordshire, Buckinghamshire, Leicestershire, Northamptonshire, Warwickshire, Worcestershire, Yorkshire

Offence, usually in the phrase *to take tut*. From Buckinghamshire: 'He took tut at it'. Someone who was usually testy, touchy, apt to take offence would be called *tutty*. From Northamptonshire: 'How tutty he is to-day'.

twanker (*noun*)

Cumberland, Lancashire, Yorkshire

A large, bulky person; anything especially large or fine. From Cumberland: 'There were two pigs charged for, a couple of twankers they are'. The adjective was *twanking*. In Yorkshire, a related word was recorded for severe, keen, or biting weather: 'A twanking frost'. The etymology isn't known; but in Lincolnshire anything very large was called a *twanger*, which may have been an earlier playful form.

twazzy (*adjective*)
Lancashire, Yorkshire

Cross, bad-tempered, irritable, quarrelsome, snappish. From Yorkshire, describing a man coming home after work: 'ill-tempered and twazzy'. He would have been in a state of *twazziness*. It's probably a variant of *twist*, as in this part of the world *twisty* was also used in the same sense. One could also *twist and twine* (from *whine*), 'be peevish'.

twickered (*adjective*)
Isle of Wight

Tired, exhausted, usually in the phrase *twickered out*. 'A must be purely twickered out wiv het [heat] and doust and drouth [dryness] and all'. The etymology is unclear, but it is probably related to *twick*, from Old English *twiccian*, 'twitch'.

twitterty-snip (*adverb*)
Devon

Restlessly, nervously. 'I marked that her fingers went twitterty-snip, just for all the world after the fashion of her tongue in days gone by'. This is *twitter* in its later (not birdsong) sense of 'tremble, be in a state of nervous apprehension', which had widespread dialect use in the British Isles and the USA. Come to think of it, that isn't too far away from the state of mind of some who use the modern social-networking service.

U

ugsome (*adjective*)

Northumberland, Scotland, Yorkshire

Disgusting, loathsome, nauseating; frightful, horrible, ghastly. From Scotland: 'An auld dog that trails its useless ugsome carcass into some bush'. 'An ugsome dream'. Loathsomeness was *ugsomeness*. A horrible sight would appear *ugsomely*. The basic element was *ug*, a verb meaning 'feel or cause disgust', derived from one of the common exclamations of distaste. As an object of disgust, one could also be an *ug*. From Northumberland: 'What an ug ye've myed yorsel'.

unfeel *or* **onfeel** (*adjective*)

Ireland, Northumberland, Scotland

Uncomfortable, unpleasant; coarse, rough. From Roxburghshire: 'An onfeel day'. 'Onfeel words'. A stronger form was *unfeelsome*. In Northumberland, the word was usually used when talking about the weather.

upping (*noun*)

Lancashire, Yorkshire

The conclusion, upshot, crisis. From Yorkshire: 'T'upping on't wor, he hed to goa' – the upshot was, he had to go. It was also used for the last hours of life, as in this old Yorkshire saw: 'We'st all ha' to come to us last uppings, if we live long enough'.

V

vady (*noun*)

† Devon, Sussex

Something carried about by a traveller to provide comforts during the journey. From Devon: 'Got something in my vady, that will make your pretty eyes flash'. It is a shortened form of *vade mecum*, Latin for 'go with me'.

viewly (*adjective*)

† Cumberland, Derbyshire, Durham, Lancashire, Lincolnshire, Northumberland, Westmorland, Yorkshire

Sightly, good to look at, handsome, comely. From Yorkshire: 'Them's as viewly a pig as onny man need wish ti see'. Even more positive would be to describe something as *viewlysome*.

vitrit *or* **vitrid** (*adjective*)

Cheshire

Angry, malicious, vicious, bitter. 'Hoo's very vitrid at him'. It's a shortened form of *inveterate*, which in its earliest recorded sense meant 'full of hatred'. In Somerset, if you were *vittery* you were quick-tempered or spiteful.

vizzy (*noun*)

Scotland

A look, a view, a scrutinizing gaze. From Edinburgh: 'We could by putting out our heads have a vizzy of the grand ancient building'. The word comes from French *visée*, 'an aim taken by using the eyes', and was much used in English when shooting at something. From Selkirkshire: 'Trying how weel they could vizy at the wild ducks'.

voxy (*adjective*)

Devon

Of the weather: deceptive, uncertain. ''Tis a voxy day tho'; but I pray the Loord to kape it off a bit'. In other words, the weather is behaving as cunningly as a fox – with a typical West Country change of *f* to *v*.

W

wab (*noun*)

† Cornwall, Devon, Lincolnshire, Somerset

The tongue – usually in the phrase *hold your wab!* But the word took on a more general meaning, as a result of not holding one's wab – 'chatter, gossip'. From Somerset: 'She an' my meesus do mostly wab together of an evening'. The etymology isn't known. It may be an echoic word, perhaps a shortened form of *babble* or *wobble* (the tongue being one of the wobbliest parts of human anatomy).

wallowish (*adjective*)

† Cumberland, Derbyshire, Durham, Gloucestershire, Herefordshire, Lancashire, Lincolnshire, Northumberland, Scotland, Westmorland, Worcestershire, Yorkshire

Insipid, tasteless; watery (of cider, beer, etc.). From Lincolnshire: 'I'd gotten no salt to put in it; it maks it a bit wallowish'. The word became even more negative when it was used for anything with a sickly or sour taste. From

Worcestershire: 'The doctor's give me some stuff as is downright wallowish; but I'm bound to saay it 'ave done me a power o' good'. It's from an Old English word, *wealg*, meaning 'insipid'.

wally *or* waly (*adjective*)

 Northumberland, Scotland

Beautiful, excellent, fine, thriving, pleasant, jolly. From Northumberland, people on a day out would be having 'a wally time'. From Scotland, Burns uses it in 'Tam o'Shanter' (l. 164): 'There was ae winsome wench and walie'. It seems to have been widely used in the North Country as a general term of admiration, but its etymology isn't known. Today, of course, *wally* as a noun (unrelated to the adjective) has acquired a totally different set of associations, as a mild term of abuse.

wambliness (*noun*)

Devon

An uneasiness or upheaval of the stomach. 'It do bring him a wambliness of the innards to do or say ought as may draw the public eye upon us'. *Wamble* – often spelled without the *b*, as *wammel*, *wommel*, and the like – was widely used in England, Scotland, and Ireland as a noun or verb to refer to food churning around or rumbling in the stomach. From Lancashire: 'Mi inside's o ov a wamble'. And if you were feeling shaky, you were all *wambly*. The origin is *wame*, a northern dialect form of *womb*, which meant 'belly' (as well as 'uterus') in Anglo-Saxon times.

wapsy (*adjective*)

Berkshire, Devon, Hampshire, Sussex, Yorkshire

Irritable, testy, ill natured, spiteful, hot tempered. From Devon: 'I won't ask 'un – her'd be wapsy with me'. It was – and still is – a common dialect pronunciation of *wasp* to reverse the *s* and the *p*.

washamouth (*noun*)

Devon, Somerset

One who blurts out anything heard; a foul-mouthed person. From Somerset: 'Don't 'ee tell her nort, her's the proper's little warshamouth ever you meet way; nif you do, 't'll be all over the town in no time'. There's clearly a link to the idiom *go wash your mouth out*, used as a reproof to someone who has used foul language or told a lie.

weeze (*verb*)

Berkshire, Cheshire, Hampshire, Lancashire, Leicestershire, Northamptonshire, Scotland, Somerset, Sussex, Warwickshire, Yorkshire

To drain away, drip gently, ooze out. From Cheshire: 'There's a spring of water weezes out from yon hill side'. From Northamptonshire: 'I'm afeard the bottle'll burst, it weezes out so at the cork'. The word is from Old English *wesan*, from *wos*, 'ooze'.

whangy (*adjective*)

Cumberland, Lancashire, Westmorland, Yorkshire

Tough, leathery. From Lancashire: 'This meat's varra whangy'. In Yorkshire *whangy cheese* was a very hard kind of cheese, made out of old milk. A *whang* was a long strip of leather, such as might be used in a shoelace or whip. The word is from Old English *þwang*, 'thong' (the initial letter was pronounced 'th').

wheem (*adjective*)

Cheshire, Cumberland, Durham, Lancashire, Lincolnshire, Northumberland, Scotland, Westmorland, Yorkshire

Pleasant, gentle, easy; soft, smooth; calm, quiet. From Westmorland: 'The machine runs very wheem when it is in good order'. In Yorkshire, calm unruffled water was described as *wheem*. The adverb *wheemly* turns up in an old Lakeland saw: 'Time gaes by, an gaes seeah whemely, Yan can nivver hear his tread'. The word is from Old English *cweman*, 'to please, delight', and was often spelled *queem*.

whemmle (*verb*)

Bedfordshire, Cumberland, Durham,
Huntingdonshire, Ireland, Lancashire, Leicestershire,
Lincolnshire, Northamptonshire, Northumberland,
Scotland, Westmorland, Yorkshire

To invert a vessel in order to cover over something.
From Yorkshire: 'I whemmeld dubler [a large bowl] owr'th
meat, To keep it seaf and warm for you'. The word was
widely used in an enormous number of spellings
(*whomble, wimmel, wummel* . . .) in many parts of the
country, especially the Midlands and North. Further
south, we find a similar word, *whelve*, with the same
meaning. It's from an Old English verb which gave rise
to *whelm* (as in *overwhelm*), 'upset, turn upside down'.
The *l* and the *m* have been transposed.

whid *or* **whud** (*noun*)

Norfolk, Scotland, Suffolk

An exaggerated statement or story, a lie, a fib. From
Kirkcudbrightshire: 'Fishers [fishermen] gets the name
o' bein fearfu fir coinin awfu [awful] whuds'. As an
earlier dictionary-writer put it: 'It conveys the idea of
less aggravation than that which is attached to the term
lie'. A brief characterization from Perthshire summar-
izes its use as a verb: 'Whiddins an airt [art]' – reflecting
the word's history, from Old English *cwide*, 'proverb,
saying'.

whimmy (*adjective*)

 Cheshire, Cornwall, Cumberland, Gloucestershire, Hampshire, Lincolnshire, Northamptonshire, Nottinghamshire, Sussex, Worcestershire, Yorkshire

Full of whims, fanciful, changeable. From Nottingham-shire: 'He's as whimmy as a dog's hairy'. From Cornwall: 'He's whiffy [changeable] and whimmy and a bit hippety-like [frivolous]'.

whud *see* whid

wibberful (*noun*)

Kent

A more easily articulated version of *wheelbarrowful*. *Wheelbarrow* itself became a *wilber* or *wibber*, used both as a noun and a verb. Try saying 'I wibber'd out a wibber-ful' in its full form and you'll sense immediately why the dialect forms evolved.

wilta-shalta (*adverb*)

Lancashire, Yorkshire

An expression of strong necessity – the equivalent of *willy-nilly*. From Lancashire: 'They lifted him clear off his feet an' carried him off wiltta shollta, whether he would or not'. The origin is 'will-to shall-to', and spellings varied greatly as writers tried to capture its different local pronunciations.

woodled (*adjective*)

⸸ Northamptonshire

Muffled, wrapped about the head and neck. 'You're so woodled up, I don't think you'll catch cold'. The etymology isn't known. The word is similar in sound to *huddle*, *mobble* ('muffle up'), *cuddle*, and other words that all seem to be expressing a sense of closeness and enclosure.

wordify (*verb*)

⸸ Devon, Yorkshire

To put into words. From Devon: ''Tiddn't no use wordifying sich acts, now things ha' changed'. If you weren't good at wordifying, you were *word-shy*. Also from Devon: 'He was never speechful, and grew more word-shy with years'.

work-brittle (*adjective*)

⸸ Cheshire, Derbyshire, Essex, Herefordshire, Lancashire, Northamptonshire, Oxfordshire, Shropshire, Staffordshire, Warwickshire, Worcestershire

Fond of work, industrious, intent upon one's work. From Warwickshire: 'I hope you feel work-brittle; there's plenty to do to-day'. The second element is a puzzle, as *brittle* normally has meanings to do with fragility and unreliability; but a comment from Cheshire gives a hint about the

possible sense development: 'Used with a sort of implication that diligence is rather unusual'.

wosbird or wuzbird (noun)
Berkshire, Gloucestershire, Hampshire, Isle of
Wight, Somerset, Sussex, Wiltshire

A term of abuse for a good-for-nothing person; also used
to children and animals. From the Isle of Wight: 'Come
out o' that ye young wuzbird, or I'll git a stick and prid
near cut ye in two'. Another sense, of 'illegitimate child',
points to the etymology – a local pronunciation of *whore's
brood*.

wostle (verb)
Cumberland, Yorkshire

To put up or obtain refreshment at an inn. 'Where do you
wostle at?' The inn would be a *wost-house*, and the host
would be the *wost*. A *wostler* was an ostler – a word that
comes from *hosteler*, a medieval word for the keeper of a
hostelry.

woubit see oobit

wudge (verb)
Yorkshire

To do anything vigorously, especially to eat voraciously.
'Aw wor wudgin' in ta sum tommy [bread and cheese] and

teea'. The etymology isn't known. The word may relate to *wedge*, in its sense of 'push in'.

wuzbird *see* **wosbird**

Y

yadder (*verb*)

Cumberland

To talk incessantly, chatter. 'Thoo yadders and talks like a gurt [great] feul'. *Ya-* was a popular source of words to do with speech – *yab*, *yack*, *yaddle*, *yaff*, *yaggle*, *yammer* . . . – all having a similar echoic origin to *gabble*, and perhaps originally related to *jaw*. The dialect use has continued in colloquial standard English to capture the notion of talk going on and on ('yada, yada, yada . . .').

yar (*adjective*)

Cumberland, Lancashire, Yorkshire

Harsh of taste, sour – also heard in *yarrish* and *yarry*, with the same meaning. From Lancashire: 'This ale's rayther yarrish'. It's a local pronunciation of *wharre*, the crab-apple, whose juice is known for its sourness. In Yorkshire, they would say that something was *as sour as wharre*.

yeeke (*verb*)

Cheshire, Yorkshire

To itch. The word was often written without the first consonant – 'I yeeke' and 'I eke' would have sounded the same. From Yorkshire: 'I eke all o'er'. The source is an Old English verb, *gyccan*, 'itch', with the *g* pronounced like a *y*, and the *cc* like *ch*.

yonderly (*adjective*)

Cheshire, Cumberland, Lancashire, Westmorland, Yorkshire

Vague, absent-minded, weak in mind or body, anxious, depressed in health or spirits. From Lancashire: 'There was a yonderly look about his eyes', 'He's look't very yonderly sin' his woife dee'd'. And if you were *far from all yonder*, you were mentally 'not all there'.

yuk out (*verb*)

Yorkshire

Of ditches: clean out, drag. A farmer had acres of potatoes under water, 'all because the authorities had not seen that the dykes had been yukked out'. The etymology is obscure, but it probably has a phonetic origin, similar to what we see in *jerk*. In several parts of the North, *yark* was used to mean 'pull something up forcibly by the roots'.

Z

zwodder (*noun*)

🕇 Somerset

A drowsy, stupid state of body or mind. The word is a local pronunciation of *swodder* or *swother*, from the Old English verb *swodrian*, whose earlier history isn't known. It well expresses the state of mind of a lexicographer who reaches the end of letter *z*.

Geographical index

This index brings together entries in this book where there is mention of a particular location within the British Isles, using designations current in 1900. For Scotland, Ireland and Wales, 'General' is used as a headword, but if an entry is illustrated by a specific location it will appear there. For example, 'daberlick' was used in many parts of Scotland, and I've chosen only the Banffshire example to illustrate it.

The number of entries in relation to each county below partly reflects the balance of coverage in Wright's Dictionary – for example, the large number of entries for Yorkshire and Scotland – but the small number of entries for some counties does not. That is simply a consequence of the items I happened to choose for this book.

England

Bedfordshire

cank, flapsy, like-shence, logaram, rightle, scrattle, smeddum, soodle, tut, whemmle

Berkshire

a-goggle, all-overish, caw-magging, drunketting, dryth, dumbfounder, ferrick, flerk, frowsty, hocksy, huckmuck, mim, misword, mulligrubs, obsteer, roomthy, shram, shucky, splute, stog, tossicated, towardly, wapsy, washamouth, weeze, wosbird

Buckinghamshire

cabby, tut

Cambridgeshire

sloum

Cheshire

abundation, anguishous, attercop, awvish, bobbersome, bogfoundered, cag-mag, cank, craichy, cramble, crumpsy, dateless, fainty, flunter, forethink, frab, fribble, frowsty, fummasing, granch, hask, izzard, kazzardly, licksome, lozzuck, mettly, misword, mortacious, motty, mulligrubs, nesh, oddlin, ponommerins, poweration, quank, quizcuss, rifty, ronkish, ronkle, scorrick, scrattle, shakaz, shalligonaked, swaggle, thrumble, tossicated, towardly, toze, tragwallet, trangleys, vitrit, weeze, wheem, whimmy, work-brittle, yeeke, yonderly

Cornwall

all-overish, backsyfore, bamfoozle, begrumpled, betwattled, buldering, buzgut, cabby, cabobble, chaffering, chilth, condiddle, confloption, corrosy, cramble, drang, dryth, dwam, fanty-sheeny, gashly, gazooly, havage, janjansy, leary, lennock, lewth, looby, mim, nesh, nickerers, niff, noggle, parwhobble,

206

perjink, pluffy, polrumptious, preedy, pussivanting, quiddle, quignogs, quob, randivoose, ronkle, sclum, scovy, scrink, shalligonaked, slawterpooch, soce, stog, suant, timdoodle, toze, wab, whimmy

Cumberland

alag, arsle, attercop, begunk, betwattled, blashy, botherment, buzznacking, chaffering, chang, clabber, cock-throppled, cramble, cronk, crottle, daggy, densh, dwam, fendy, frab, hask, havey-cavey, illify, izzard, kenspeck, kysty, lorricker, mattery, middlemer, muckment, nang, nazzard, nesh, nunty, otherguess, oxter, peedle, pload, plook, prickmedainty, rackups, radgy, rifty, rightle, sang, scorrick, scrattle, scroggins, scrunty, scumfish, sillified, slench, sloum, sot-whol, stime, strunt, stuffment, swaggle, tawm, tharfish, thrumble, torfle, tossicated, towardly, toze, trangleys, twanker, viewly, wallowish, whangy, wheem, whemmle, whimmy, wostle, yadder, yar, yonderly

Derbyshire

all-overish, awvish, barkle, cank, craichy, cramble, dateless, frab, granch, hask, havey-cavey, heigh-go-mad, izzard, licksome, motty, nesh, oobit, oxter, puckeration, rifty, scorrick, scrattle, slamp, splawt, tossicated, towardly, viewly, wallowish, work-brittle

Devon

alkitotle, apurt, backsyfore, baltiorum, begrumpled, betwattled, boneshave, botherment, briss, broodle, buldering, buzznacking, cabby, cag-mag, capadocious, click-ma-doodle, condiddle, corrosy, doaty, drang,

dryth, dumbfounder, dwam, fainty, fanty-sheeny,
gangagous, gashly, harriage, havage, huckmuck,
jobbernowl, leary, lennock, lewth, mang, mulligrubs,
nesh, niff, otherguess, parwhobble, pluffy,
pussivanting, puzzomful, randivoose, ronkle, sclum,
scovy, scrawlation, shazzaas, slawterpooch, soce,
squinch, steehop, stog, suant, taffety, tossicated, toze,
trangleys, twitterty-snip, vady, voxy, wab, wambliness,
wapsy, washamouth, wordify

Dorset

drang, dryth, flob, funch, huckmuck, leary, lennock,
lewth, limbless, misword, nang, nesh, pious-high,
quiddle, quob, scorrick, shalligonaked, shram, soce,
stog, suant, taffety, trangleys

Durham

argh, argle, awvish, blashy, bowdykite, crottle, daggy,
densh, dwam, fendy, grob, hettle, izzard, kenspeck,
mang, mim, oobit, oxter, proggle, pross, rifty, sang,
scumfish, slench, sloum, smeddum, stime, thrawn,
torfle, viewly, wallowish, wheem, whemmle

Essex

bange, chice, hainish, jounce, lab-dab, limpsy,
mulligrubs, work-brittle

Gloucestershire

abundation, aizam-jazam, bathy, cag-mag,
caw-magging, cusnation, darricky, doppet, drang,
dryth, dwam, fainty, flimp, frack, frowsty, glat, granch,
gurly, hocksy, izzard, lewth, maggle, misword, nesh,
niff, quank, quiddle, quob, ronkish, rox, sang, scorrick,

scrigs, shram, shucky, suant, swaggle, tossicated,
towardly, trimple, tush, wallowish, whimmy, wosbird

Hampshire

a-goggle, cusnation, drang, dryth, dumbfounder, flerk,
funch, glox, huckmuck, jawbation, leary, lennock,
lewth, limpsy, mulligrubs, nesh, noggle, quiddle,
scorrick, shram, shucky, soce, squit, stog, suant,
taffety, wapsy, weeze, whimmy, wosbird

Herefordshire

abundation, addle, fainty, glat, gurly, jammock, keffel,
lewth, licksome, misword, nesh, parsed, parwhobble,
poweration, quabble, quank, quob, rainified, ronkish,
rox, shucky, snaff, tossicated, towardly, trimple, tush,
wallowish, work-brittle

Hertfordshire

bange, bluify, hainish, lerry

Huntingdonshire

drowk, jawbation, picklick, soodle, whemmle

Isle of Wight

drang, dryth, funch, lerry, lewth, limbless, quiddle,
quob, rox, shram, skitterways, suant, swotchel, taffety,
tossicated, twickered, wosbird

Kent

addle, bathy, boldrumptious, bruff, cag-mag,
chaffering, dryth, ernful, fawnicate, lewth, misword,
mortacious, nang, nunty, polrumptious, shucky,
slonky, spong, taffety, wibberful

Lancashire

all-overish, anguishous, arsle, attercop, awvish, barkle,

betwattled, bobbersome, brackle, bruff,
buck-thwanging, cag-mag, cank, ceffle, chaffering,
chang, cheeping-merry, cramble, daggy, dateless,
dwam, fendy, flunter, forethink, frab, fubsy,
fummasing, granch, hask, havey-cavey, heigh-go-mad,
illify, izzard, jobbernowl, kazzardly, kenspeck,
kobnoggle, kysty, licksome, lorricker, lozzuck,
madancholy, motty, muckment, nazzard, nesh, oxter,
paamus, partick, peedle, puckeration, puzzomful,
rainified, rifty, rightle, saidment, sang, scarcify,
scorrick, scrattle, scrunty, sidth, slamp, slench, sloum,
smittling, spaw, sticklebutt, stime, strollop,
tanklements, tawm, thusk, torfle, towardly, twanker,
twazzy, upping, viewly, wallowish, wambliness, weeze,
whangy, wheem, whemmle, wilta-shalta, work-brittle,
yar, yonderly

Leicestershire

blashy, braddled, cank, craichy, crimpledy, feelth,
flimp, frowsty, gashly, granch, mang, nesh, nunty,
oddlin, pluffy, proggle, queechy, quob, rifty, roomthy,
rox, scrattle, snaff, snozy, splatherdab, toldrum,
towardly, tut, weeze, whemmle

Lincolnshire

all-overish, argh, argle, baggerment, barkle,
batterfanged, bemoil, blashy, blutterbunged, brackle,
broodle, cag-mag, chaffering, chollous, craichy,
cramble, crimpledy, dateless, densh, doggery-baw,
dottled, eardly, grob, hask, havey-cavey, illify, izzard,
jawbation, jawmotry, jobbernowl, kenspeck,

lally-wow, lerry, mang, muckment, mulligrubs, nesh,
nunty, obsteer, oddlin, peedle, polrumptious, pross,
quizcuss, radgy, rifty, rightle, sang, scorrick, scranky,
scumfish, semi-demi, shucky, slod, sloum, smittling,
soodle, stitherum, struncheon, thusk, toldrum, toze,
twanker, viewly, wab, wallowish, wheem, whemmle,
whimmy

London
chaffering, flerk

Middlesex
rainified, tantrups

Norfolk
addle, arsle, bange, brackle, bruff, cabobble,
cag-mag, chamble, chice, confloption, daggy, densh,
discomfrontle, frack, fribble, gadwaddick, grut,
gruttling, harriage, jammock, jawbation, jounce,
kedgy, lab-dab, lig, limpsy, mawbish, mim,
mortacious, mulligrubs, nunty, pample, parsed,
qualmified, quezzen, sammodithee, scorrick, scrink,
shram, shucky, sidth, sillified, slod, snickup, squit,
swaggle, trangleys, whid

Northamptonshire
baltiorum, betwattled, blashy, brackle, cank,
caw-magging, chamble, crimpledy, cumpuffled,
discomfrontle, drowk, dumbfounder, feelth, ferrick,
frack, frowsty, giddling, harriage, havey-cavey,
izzard, jawbation, like-shence, logaram, mang,
miscomfrumple, nesh, nunty, oddlin, partick, pload,
proggle, qualmified, roomthy, rox, scorrick, scrunty,

seemth, skenchback, soodle, splatherdab, towardly,
tut, weeze, whemmle, whimmy, woodled, work-brittle

Northumberland

aclite, alag, argh, attercop, barkle, betwattled, birthy,
blashy, bobbersome, boodyankers, bowdykite, cadgy,
cag-mag, camsteery, cogglety, cramble, crottle, daggy,
densh, dowpy, dwam, fandandering, fendy, gurly, hettle,
izzard, jawbation, kenspeck, lab-dab, lobstropolous,
longcanny, mang, mattery, mim, nesh, nunty, oobit,
oxter, pload, plook, prickmedainty, prinkling, proggle,
radgy, rumgumption, sang, scrunty, scumfish, slonky,
sloum, snoove, snot-snorl, sprunt, stime, strunt,
tharfish, tiny-tiny, toober, torfle, ugsome, unfeel,
viewly, wallowish, wally, wheem, whemmle

Nottinghamshire

barkle, cag-mag, cank, chamble, craichy, cramble,
cronk, flimp, frowsty, granch, hagg, havey-cavey,
modge, mulligrubs, nesh, nunty, oddlin, radgy, rifty,
rightle, ronkish, scorrick, shucky, sloum, thusk,
tiff-taffle, toldrum, whimmy

Oxfordshire

fainty, ferrick, flob, frowsty, giddling, hocksy,
jawbation, maggle, mim, mulligrubs, norman, quob,
roomthy, sillified, sprunt, swotchel, trickumtrully,
work-brittle

Rutland

feelth, logaram, odocity, rightle, soodle

Shropshire

abundation, aizam-jazam, awvish, backsyfore, bathy,

bobbersome, broodle, cag-mag, cank, chamble,
craichy, frowsty, glat, granch, jammock, jurgy,
kazzardly, keffel, kenspeck, lozzuck, mulligrubs,
nesh, niff, noggle, norman, nunty, oddlin, onshooty,
parwhobble, poweration, quank, quob, ronkish,
scrattle, shalligonaked, shupernacular, sidth, splawt,
swaggle, tossicated, towardly, toze, trimple, tush,
work-brittle

Somerset

abbey-lubber, all-overish, apurt, bamfoozle,
begrumpled, betwattled, boneshave, botherment,
briss, buldering, buzznacking, cabby, certy, condiddle,
doaty, drang, dryth, fanty-sheeny, gurly, jawbation,
keffel, larmy, leary, lennock, lewth, limbless, linnard,
mang, mulligrubs, nang, nesh, niff, otherguess,
queechy, scarcify, scorrick, scovy, shakaz, shram,
slawterpooch, soce, steehop, stog, suant, taffety,
tossicated, toze, vitrit, wab, washamouth, weeze,
wosbird, zwodder

Staffordshire

abundation, aizam-jazam, awvish, bemoil, brackle,
cank, craichy, cramble, giddling, hask, illify, knivy,
lozzuck, nesh, poweration, queechy, ronkish, scorrick,
splute, work-brittle

Suffolk

addle, arsle, bange, brackle, bruff, cabobble, cag-mag,
chamble, chice, confloption, daggy, discomfrontle,
finnying, flimp, frack, fribble, gashly, gruttling,
harriage, izzard, jammock, jobbernowl, jounce,

kedgy, lab-dab, lig, limpsy, mawbish, mim, misword,
mortacious, mulligrubs, norman, nunty, oxter,
pample, quezzen, randivoose, sammodithee, scorrick,
scrink, shucky, sillified, slod, snickup, squit, swaggle,
trangleys, whid

Surrey

addle, chocketty, dryth, lewth, misword, niff,
rainified, shucky, sillified, skitterways, someness,
spong, taffety

Sussex

addle, argh, bowzelly, brabagious, bruff, camsteery,
dryth, dumbfounder, ernful, fawnicate, gashly,
jawbation, leary, lennock, lewth, limpsy, misword,
mortacious, mulligrubs, nang, niff, nunty, pettigues,
quiddle, shram, shucky, skitterways, spong, suant,
taffety, vady, wapsy, weeze, whimmy, wosbird

Warwickshire

aizam-jazam, all-overish, argle, awvish, bemoil,
blashy, cag-mag, cank, chamble, craichy,
dumbfounder, fainty, feelth, ferrick, flimp, fribble,
frowsty, gashly, giddling, granch, hask, jawbation,
keffel, misword, modge, mortacious, motty,
mulligrubs, nesh, nunty, oddlin, pluffy, proggle,
quank, queechy, ronkish, roomthy, rox, scorrick,
scrattle, shram, soodle, splatherdab, squit, swaggle,
toldrum, tossicated, tut, weeze, work-brittle

Westmorland

attercop, blodder, bobbersome, botherment, brittner,
bruff, chaffering, chang, cock-throppled, cogglety,

cramble, cronk, crottle, dateless, flaup, frab, glat,
glorys, goddle-house, illify, kenspeck, kysty, lorricker,
middlemer, mome, nang, nazzard, nesh, nurble, oxter,
parsed, peedle, proggle, rackups, rainified, rifty,
rightle, scorrick, scroggins, scumfish, skurreboloo,
slench, sloum, sot-whol, stime, stuffment, torfle,
tossicated, trangleys, viewly, wallowish, whangy,
wheem, whemmle, yonderly

Wiltshire

attercop, cank, cusnation, drang, flerk, flob, frowsty,
gashly, glox, harriage, hocksy, huckmuck, izzard,
lewth, mang, misword, mulligrubs, nesh, otherguess,
pussivanting, quank, quiddle, quob, ronkish, scrigs,
shram, shucky, soce, stog, suant, taffety, towardly,
wosbird

Worcestershire

abundation, aizam-jazam, argle, bathy, begrumpled,
bencher, bruff, cackle-stomached, cag-mag, cank,
craichy, crimpledy, dimracker, fainty, feelth, flimp,
frowsty, gadwaddick, gashly, giddling, glat, granch,
keffel, leary, maggle, misword, nesh, parsed, quank,
quiddle, quob, ronkish, rox, scorrick, scrigs, shobble,
shucky, slench, toober, trimple, tush, tut, wallowish,
whimmy, work-brittle

Yorkshire

abbey-lubber, adawds, alag, aptish, argh, arse-verse,
arsle, attercop, awvish, baltiorum, bamfoozle, barkle,
batterfanged, bazzock, beflum, beraffled, betwattled,
betwittered, blashy, bobbersome, botherment,

boundsy, bowdykite, brackle, brittner, bruff, buck-thwanging, buzznacking, cadgy, cag-mag, capadocious, catty-bargle, chaffering, chollous, cogglety, cramble, crimpledy, cronk, crottle, daggy, danglements, dateless, densh, derrum, dumbfounder, dwam, fainty, fendy, flaup, flob, flunter, forethink, frab, fribble, fubsy, glorys, granch, grob, grumptious, hask, havey-cavey, heigh-go-mad, hengments, hettle, illify, ireful, izzard, jawbation, jawmotry, jobbernowl, jubbity, kazzardly, keffel, kenspeck, kysty, lab-dab, lassified, lennock, licksome, longcanny, lorricker, lumrified, madancholy, mang, middlemer, mim, misword, mome, motty, muckment, mulligrubs, nang, nazzard, nesh, noggle, norman, nunty, oamly, obsteer, oddlin, otherguess, oxter, partick, peedle, pettigues, pload, plook, pluffy, pross, puckeration, puzzomful, radgy, rainified, rifty, rightle, ronkish, roomthy, rumgumption, ryntle, saidment, scaum, scorrick, scranky, scrattle, scrunty, scumfish, sheddle, shivvy, sidth, skenchback, slamp, slench, sloonge, sloum, smeddum, smittling, snickup, soodle, spaw, steg, sticklebutt, stime, stirriner, stramash, strollop, struncheon, suddenty, sumph, swid, swip, tanklements, tawm, tharfish, thring, thruffable, thrumble, thrung, tiddytoit, toldrum, torfle, tossicated, trangleys, tush, tut, twanker, twazzy, ugsome, upping, viewly, wallowish, wapsy, weeze, whangy, wheem, whemmle, whimmy, wilta-shalta, wordify, wostle, wudge, yar, yeeke, yonderly, yuk out

Ireland

General

amplush, ashiepattle, attercop, begunk, blashy,
bruff, cadgy, chice, clabber, cogglety, dowpy, dwam,
fandandering, gurly, hask, kenspeck, lewth, mim,
oxter, proggle, rifty, rightle, sang, scarcify, scrunty,
sloum, snaggilty, strunt, surree, tragwallet, unfeel,
wambliness, whemmle

Northern Ireland

General

birthy, rickmatick, slonky, stime, thrawn

Scotland

General

aclite, afflufe, alunt, argle, arse-verse, attercop,
awvish, bangster, beflum, begrumpled, begunk,
birthy, blaff, blashy, blawp, blodder, brabagious,
cattie-bargle, chaffering, chang, clabber, cloffin,
cogglety, cognost, condiddle, daggy, dixie-fixie,
dottled, dowpy, dumbfounder, fainty, fendy, flob,
forethink, fribble, glox, gurly, hask, hettle, huckmuck,
izzard, jobbernowl, keffel, kenspeck, lassified, mang,

mettly, mim, mulligrubs, mumple, nesh, nickerers,
novels, oobit, oxter, perqueer, pleep, pload, plouk,
pluffy, proggle, rifty, scoll, scorrick, scranky, scrunty,
slonky, sloum, snaff, solemncholy, stime, stramash,
suddenty, surree, swip, tawm, tharfish, thrawn, toober,
torfle, tragwallet, trangleys, ugsome, wallowish, wally,
wambliness, weeze, wheem, whemmle

Aberdeenshire

argh, glack, orp, perqueer, rumgumption, scouk,
solacious, sumph, swick, toot-moot

Ayrshire

bumbaze, cadgy, prickmedainty, prinkling, splute,
terrification

Banffshire

curglaff, daberlick, perqueer, sclatch, swick, thrumble

Berwickshire

camsteery

Dumfriesshire

sang, snoove, snozy, thring

Edinburgh

snoove, vizzy

Fife

camsteery, footer-footer

Forfarshire (Angus)

perjink, ramfeezled, rickmatick

Galloway (Wigtownshire)

noof, steg

Kirkcudbrightshire

noof, whid

Lanarkshire
noof
Lothian
blup, chorp, dwam, scumfish
Orkney and Shetland Isles
ashiepattle, cataclue, deepooperit, finnying, mirligo,
oob, pleep, snyirk, tud
Perthshire
camsteery, preedy, whid
Renfrewshire
crottle, deceivery, novels
Roxburghshire
unfeel
Selkirkshire
bowzelly, prinkling, skype, smeddum, strunt, vizzy

Isle of Man

oxter, rackups, rifty, tossicated

Wales

General
awvish, cank, drang, dryth, glat, keffel, licksome, nesh,
strollop, suant
Cardigan
rasmws

Glamorgan
coppish
Pembrokeshire
amplush, hummy, lumrified, noggle, roomthy

Have they disappeared?

Joseph Wright was recording usages from the late 1800s. A century on, are any of these words and expressions still being used in the counties named? Or are any of them being used in places other than the ones he reported – either within or beyond the British Isles?

These pages provide a space to make notes of any present-day occurrences of items that match those listed in this book. Spellings often vary, but make sure that the sense of an item corresponds to the one presented in the entry. If possible, note the source of when and where you heard or saw it used.

If you add the information to the *Disappearing Dictionary* website, we can build up a nationwide picture of whether any of these old words have survived. Go to:

www.disappearingdictionary.com

Word or expression

Where did you find it?

Source details

Word or expression

Where did you find it?

Source details

Word or expression

Where did you find it?

Source details

Word or expression

Where did you find it?

Source details

Word or expression

Where did you find it?

Source details

Word or expression

Where did you find it?

Source details

Word or expression

Where did you find it?

Source details

Word or expression

Where did you find it?

Source details

Word or expression

Where did you find it?

Source details

Word or expression

Where did you find it?

Source details

Word or expression

Where did you find it?

Source details

Word or expression

Where did you find it?

Source details